Praise For *The Secrets of the Hidden Workforce*

Ms. Toth tells compelling stories with compassion and respect about real people who struggle, enjoy life, cry when they are mistreated and celebrate achieving their wildest dreams. Her book is a testimony to the fact that people with disabilities want the same things that everyone wants and that they too deserve to live productive lives with the potential to benefit society and themselves through contributions to the workforce and their communities.

　–Melinda Fruendt, Executive Director, Division of Rehabilitation
　Services Oklahoma

A few words that describe Lisa and Rise Staffing are; determination, resourcefulness, patience and caring. Our journey with Lisa dates back to the early 2000s and during this time, my daughter Laurie has gone from an out of control special needs teenager with no direction or self esteem to a mature special needs person who is confident, outgoing and able to work independently outside of funded employment & contribute to society in many ways greater than some without special needs.

　–Alex Winiecke, Customer Parent

Author Lisa Toth is dedicated to finding meaningful work and purpose for people with varying abilities. With her boutique style staffing company, she always treats each individual with the utmost respect. I hope you enjoy this book as much as I did....

　–Dawn and Autumn Butler, Mom and Daughter Advocates

This book shows how brave Lisa Toth actually is. Not only is Lisa sharing her truth, she is embracing her vulnerability. However uncomfortable it is to expose one's true self with flaws Lisa shares hers with authenticity...

–Daniele Hillyer LSC LPPC

I have known Lisa for more than 15 years and found her book an enjoyable read of her life-long history working with individuals with disabilities. She has an unwavering commitment to this clientele, and continues to make a positive impact in the lives of those who she shares her talents with. Lisa's work has made an impact in her state and community. Lisa's initiative, enthusiasm and passion are like none other in the field. From political education and awareness to her innovative partnerships with agencies and employers, she always gives 1000 percent.

—Lisa DeBolt, Parent Advocate, satisfied customer

THE
SECRETS
OF
THE HIDDEN
WORKFORCE

Yorkshire Publishing
TULSA

ISBN: 978-1-960810-40-3
The Secrets of The Hidden Workforce
Copyright © 2023 by Lisa Toth
All rights reserved.

Yorkshire Publishing
1425 E 41st Pl
Tulsa, OK 74105
www.YorkshirePublishing.com
918.394.2665

Published in Canada
Printed in Canada

THE SECRETS OF THE HIDDEN WORKFORCE

By Lisa Toth

FOREWARD

A good part of her success is due to her sense of humor. Lisa always gravitates back to happiness and fun. Our business can be challenging and sometimes not so fun. A smile and a laugh makes what we do more positive and effective.

I'm older now and 30 years ago Lisa was a kid. To me she still is. She has young energy while remaining committed to serious outcomes like legislative work, developing a successful agency and surfacing as a solid base for people in need.

For years we have talked about our shared outlook and philosophy. That is, if we do our jobs effectively, eventually we won't be needed. That seems a strange thing to look forward to, but it is an honorable vision. Not everyone can embrace this notion. Some find it unbelievable. Lisa sees it as a goal. Timely developments and new ideas are what Lisa thrives on. Her movement through the disability world is enviable. If you have an opportunity to meet Lisa, do yourself a favor and spend time with her. If not, pay attention to what she has written on these pages or says on her radio show. That will give you an idea of the magic of Lisa Toth.

John DePaula
Retired DD Professional
Life time Advocate

Contents

INTRODUCTION

I have written *The Secrets of the Hidden Workforce* to tell the story of how I came to create the Rise Staffing agency based on my experience working with developmentally disabled individuals. I wanted to share some of the lessons I've learned over the course of my career, and to describe how the agency's services have been able to help many thousands of individuals with disabilities find work that is a good fit for their abilities, and that they find fulfilling.

Individuals with special needs have often experienced discrimination both in the workplace and in their daily lives. Growing up, my own parents went so far as to forbid me from even interacting with them. As a result of this prejudice, these individuals can have difficulty finding jobs; when they do get work, they are often given menial tasks, and are isolated from or shunned by other workers who find it easy to consider them inferior.

However, with training and social support, developmentally disabled individuals can learn to use their skills to do many types of jobs successfully—and find fulfillment and social acceptance in the process. I have long worked with such individuals as a job coach because I have been inspired by the success stories of many developmentally disabled people.

As a result of my work experience and desire to help disabled individuals, in 2004 I opened the Phoenix Residential Services agency in order to help my clients live and learn as part of the broader community. Later, I recreated my agency as Rise Staffing in order to help these individuals find great jobs. I did so because of my lifelong experience and the inspiration I found in seeing individuals with special needs achieve success. I also felt that doing what I could to help them live meaningful and productive lives was an essential service that contributed to the well-being of society by helping marginalized people realize their own potential.

I've spent the majority of my life trying to satisfy my internal burning desire to open the eyes of the general public to the daily struggles and intricate lives of people with different abilities. We often hear in society about how they're valued—usually as part of wonderful "human-interest" stories. Especially when it comes to the extraordinary things that people can do with limited bodily resources or mental capacity. But one-off news stories aren't the same as real understanding and acceptance. That's the kind of story I want to tell.

This book is dedicated to all the people that I have been involved with over the years—to those I've loved, admired, liked, disliked, and grown with. Yes, even to the people I've disliked; I'm not gonna lie, because you know life isn't fair, and you just don't jive with everybody. But that doesn't mean it's not possible to learn from one another, and to value parts of what you experienced. Sometimes I think that's the biggest criticism I receive—how I always try to put a positive spin on things, no matter what the issue is...

Anyway, in order to tell my story, I feel that I first need to go back to my childhood, as that's when the seeds of everything that would come later were sown.

Growing up in the sixties and seventies as the oldest of three, I remember being free to use my imagination. This was especially true whenever I was around my little sister and brother; I felt safe and free with those two. We played in the woods, built forts, climbed trees—and sometimes got to watch television.

During kindergarten and first grade, Nana Toth babysat me after school. The game shows and soap operas we watched together shaped my young mind. *Dark Shadows, Ryan's Hope, All My Children, One Life to Live*, and the finale at 3 p.m. EST—*General Hospital!* Of course, dear reader, as you can imagine, little Lisa was not sitting still through all these programs. I was constantly running in and out, playing, whatever—but if I was near that box, my eyes and ears were glued to ABC daytime programming.

There's a lot to learn from soap opera stories. Watching families play out their intricate relationships between commercial breaks fascinated and hooked me at the early age of four. Maybe Nana didn't realize I was absorbing her stories. I'm glad she let me watch them with her. I really love you, Nana Toth.

Those TV people were friends to Nana and me. Sometimes Nana would have a friend over, and they would yak about the stories and their theories about plots. I loved every minute of those conversations; usually eating a cookie and sipping a cup of tea with milk and sugar, I smiled and listened and made mental notes.

At one point in my adolescence, my siblings and I played *General Hospital*. What? Yep, that's right—we played a soap opera. Here's how we did it. Each one of us decided our characters—I was usually Dr. Monica Quartermaine. The theme was determined by our immediate surroundings. For instance, if we were outside at our family's pool, we pretended we were on vacation in Hawaii. We just made up our dialogue based on the current storyline.

My sister was Dr. Leslie Webber, (only because Susan Lucci's Erica Kane was on *All My Children*) and my little brother played Dr. Jeff Martin. We were precious and hilarious, us three. We were strongly bonded throughout our childhood.

Standing up for my younger siblings came naturally to me; you may not be surprised to learn that I often got in trouble for standing up for others in school! I realized early on that no one in charge cared about the injustices, even the bullying, that I was reporting to them. Well, I couldn't allow injustice and bullying to continue while I was around. Five-year-old me decided to take matters into my own hands. Huh? I was five years old—what was I going to do? Here's what I came up with; it was a strategy I continued to practice up until fifth grade.

1. Ask the bully to stop whatever mean thing they were doing.
2. Tell them they better stop.
3. One more verbal warning while I got madder.
4. The "Tothy Punch."*
5. Yeah, that's right, don't pick on my little sister.

Note: The Tothy punch was and is not a good idea, and is not endorsed by the author—do not do this.

I balled my fist and turned it sideways and tomahawk-punched them on the back between their shoulders. The Tothy punch was pretty a powerful statement against what I deemed injustice.

Sadly, it took a long time for me to realize that I, too, had become a bully. It started with good intentions to protect people who couldn't protect themselves. Over time, I got a reputation, which was exciting—a tiny taste of popularity and power.

A new girl entered my school when I was in fifth grade. She and I tangled—over what, I can't remember; what I do remember is that she quickly punched me in the face and knocked me down. I got up, and vowed to never use the Tothy punch on another person.

Around the same time, my babysitter told me that if I Tothy punched a kid while their eyes were crossed, their eyes would stay crossed forever.

Geez, I didn't want to be responsible for disabling someone! Yikes, crossed eyes forever? I tried to keep my eyes crossed for as long as I could; I needed to see what it would be like for the poor kid who just happened to be crossing his eyes as I punched him. Horrible. I couldn't live with myself for causing such disfigurement. And I would probably see the kid in school all the time. A constant reminder of my maiming ways. Every time I was in the hallways the cross-eyed kid would be there, and I would not even be able to tell if he was looking at me. No, I couldn't take the guilt that came with this new horrible potential consequence my babysitter had laid on me. So the Tothy Punch was permanently retired.

But seriously, I knew there were plenty of ways other than physical assault to deal with bullies. I'm grateful that girl's family moved to my school district in my fifth-grade year. The girl's punch was impactful, and it allowed me to change course.

The other lesson I learned is that people who are able to make changes that could prevent injustices will often ignore information that should open their eyes, even when you clearly bring problems to their attention.

One of the phrases you will hear from me often is "Ants can move rubber tree plants." You may remember the song, and the little black-and-white cartoon with ants pulling rubber tree plants out with a cute little popping sound. "Whoops, there goes another rubber tree plant!" I loved it when I was a child and I still do, because I've got high hopes—"high, apple-pie-in-the-sky hopes."

Whenever I feel beat down, like I just can't do it anymore—ants start moving rubber tree plants, and the melody gets in my head, and a smile takes over, and we find another way!

Currently, there are really weird things happening in today's society—political things that I cannot understand happening, things that I was not raised to believe in. I'm not talking about any kind of party politics. I'm talking about simple truths and lies. When I was a kid, I learned how George Washington could not tell a lie. He chopped down that cherry tree, but he told the truth even though he risked punishment. I took that little cherry tree story to heart and kept it with me. Then I learned about not lying when I went to Sunday school at church. Throughout this book you'll hear me talk about the lesson my parents taught me—just be honest, and I'll back you up. But how can you back somebody up if you don't know whether they're telling you the truth—or if they even care?

This makes me concerned about the work that we've done to help people with different abilities become more included in society. What does it mean if that society is dangerously contaminated with half-truths? We've helped people get out of institutional living environments and into their communities—communities where discrimination, unkind words, and murder are common occurrences. That's right, murder! People are being murdered just because somebody doesn't like the way they look, or because somebody had a bad day, or is mad at a teacher, doctor, boss, or co-worker. Bam, they shoot them. Any day they could target people with developmental or other disabilities, and it terrifies me that this may happen.

I want people to know how valuable every life is—and act like it. Here in the great state of Oklahoma, there is absolutely zero tolerance for abortion, and people believe that life begins at conception. If that's the case, then it means that *everybody* who lives here should be respected and treated the exact same way and have the exact same rights and access to the exact same services. But that's not the case— which is the reason why I'm telling these stories.

Many of us have somebody in our family with a different ability, or know somebody who does. It's easier to understand issues when they're close to home. But why does it have to be like that? Why can't we care for people in our community even if we're not directly connected to them? Many groups in our society have a tendency to exclude people they don't like—that is, people who aren't like them. I don't want people with disabilities to be included in all that again. They and their allies have fought for their rights, to get out of institutions, to become included, to gain voter accessibility. This is serious business, and I want to be clear about the stakes here.

I also want to make it clear to readers that certain places, names, and other details in this book have been fictionalized for legal reasons. However, I have experienced and worked at places that are very similar to everything referenced in these pages. I'm not naming them because I didn't have legal rights and I don't want to break any kind of confidentiality.

Also, I want to acknowledge all of the people who have worked for me and with me in the past. I appreciate everything that you've done, and all the things you've taught me. I've learned so much from all of you and you will always have a good place in my heart—unless you stabbed me in the back.

This book features the stories of many people whom I have found especially inspiring, because of the ways they have been able to succeed despite having to overcome so many challenges in their path.

PART I

CREATING AN AGENCY
TO INSPIRE PEOPLE

CHAPTER 1

How Job Coaching People With Developmental And Other Disabilities Became My Life Art

I came to the work I am doing now—coaching people with developmental and other disabilities to find fulfilling work—due to experiences I had when I was growing up and getting started on my career path. Along the way, I found my life's calling and purpose in doing this work. That is what eventually led me to create Rise Staffing, which helps developmentally disabled people as its mission. I call this my life art!

This chapter describes how I came to develop this mission for myself, and for the agency.

Beginnings

The beginning of my journey can be traced back to my early childhood, to the first time I met a person with different abilities. This had a profound effect on my perspective on life.

This encounter happened when I was four years old, living in a middle-income suburban neighborhood. The neighbors down the street had a child named Johnny, who people referred to as "mongoloid"—an outdated and insensitive term that refers to a supposed Asian-like appearance sometimes associated with Down syndrome.

Of course, I didn't understand that at the time, nor did I understand why Johnny was only able to communicate by making grunt-like sounds, another trait associated with his condition, which was severe.

Although I did not know it at the time, this syndrome is due to a genetic disorder that occurs when abnormal cell division results in extra genetic material from chromosome twenty-one. People with this condition have a distinct facial appearance, an intellectual disability, and developmental delays. However, thanks to tireless advocacy efforts, today many people with Down syndrome are able to be successful in a wide variety of jobs, including supermarket clerks and working with animals.

After I met Johnny, my parents, like many people who reject and seek to avoid being around developmentally disabled individuals, told me to stay away from him because he looked different from other children and could not speak like them. But I did not think my parents had a good reason for my not being friends with Johnny, and their reaction only made me more curious to find out more about him. Eventually, we ended up becoming good friends.

As I got to know Johnny, I came to understand his special language and we found ways to communicate. Though he was different from other children and saw the world in a unique way, he wasn't scary to me at all. When I first met him, he rattled the chain link fence around his house and made some grunting noises. I figured he just wanted to get my attention, so I went over to him. I remember laughing and dancing with him through the fence. After a few days, Johnny's mom noticed us together, and she invited me in and offered me chocolate chip cookies. After that, I continued to visit Johnny and found him a warm, loving person. I liked spending time with him. Soon after that, though, my family moved away. I never saw Johnny again, though he made an enormous impact on me.

That early experience helped to kindle my desire to understand and help developmentally disabled people. Experiences I had as I continued to grow up—and later, when I entered the workforce—only reinforced the outlook I developed as a young child.

Turning a Desire to Help People into a Career Path

As I grew up, I felt a powerful desire to help people. I began my career doing this work when I joined the Doylestown ARC as a direct support staff member in 1980. I was eighteen years old. The ARC is an organization that is committed to promoting and protecting the human rights of people with intellectual and developmental disabilities, and it actively supports their full inclusion and participation in the community throughout their life. There are local chapters of the organization all over the country.

I started working for the ARC when I was studying at an agricultural school, where I learned about the genetic breeding of hogs. Though I loved studying animals, I was even more interested in helping people, and my work at the ARC helped to confirm that this was the right career path for me.

My job at the ARC involved assisting three women who lived in an apartment with their personal care staff. My responsibilities included teaching them everyday skills like shopping and going to a bank. Also, I helped them become integrated into their community in numerous ways. Among other things, the Doylestown ARC sponsored a Special Olympics program, and the three women participated in bowling and track events. I especially appreciated their "never-give-up attitude." One time, I took them to visit my college dairy farm, and one woman was even able to milk a cow. I met many individuals in the program, and I found it truly inspiring to see the way they were accepted. I also appreciated the arduous work of the ARC staff members in supporting extremely disabled athletes and helping them compete.

I worked with the ARC for three years, and I found the work very fulfilling as I saw these women develop the skills and self-assurance to adjust successfully in their daily lives. I became friends with them as well. In turn, this experience helped me solidify the decision I had made to work in the helping profession, and to help individuals who were developmentally disabled live more satisfying lives.

Working as a Direct Care Worker and House Manager

Then, in 1983, when I was twenty-one, I became a direct care worker for the New Jersey Institution. I worked in a hospital ward in an institutional setting that cared for residents with a high need for medical care. The hospital had four different wards, each one supervised by a registered nurse and service workers like me. My shift was from 3 to 11 p.m.

All the wards had permanent, total care residents—except my ward, Ward A, which provided temporary care for any residents of the campus who became ill, were back from the hospital, were recovering from an injury, or otherwise required nursing assistance. In addition to assisting the RN, I worked with another direct care staff member, Ms. B. She had been working at the hospital for eighteen years, so she had seniority over the other employees. She frequently talked about her rights as a member of AFSCME, the American Federation of State, County, and Municipal Employees—the largest trade union of public employees in the United States, as she was quick to remind everyone.

Until I worked at this institution, I had never experienced so many disabled people together at one time. I also saw many representations of disabled people during my training, when the instructor showed us photos of many of the institution's residents and explained the many disabilities of the people we would be treating.

Once I began working there, I saw people who were living with disabilities that I had never imagined. For example, Violet had the most extreme case of pica I've ever seen, which led her to have many surgeries because of all the inedible things she ate. Pica is a compulsive eating disorder in which people eat non-food items—most commonly dirt, clay, and flaking paint, as well as glue, hair, cigarette ashes, and feces. Before I began working at the hospital, Violet had already had many surgeries; I was shocked by the appearance of her body when I began performing intimate personal care on her. I saw at least eight long, vertical cuts on her torso, which had me choking back tears. The surgeries had been done to remove indigestible things she had eaten, including a dead bird and an entire bed sheet, which almost killed her because it was so big.

Violet's intestines had been damaged from repeated surgery, so most of the time whatever she ate came out in liquid form. Also, because there were only two staff people and a nurse to care for her, it was not possible to observe her at all times, so she had to wear a specially designed helmet to prevent her from eating. The helmet had a plexiglass cover that was stitched on with some shoelace string and laced up in the back, so it looked like a boxing glove. The plexiglass had little air holes drilled into it so she could breathe, but it prevented her from putting anything in her mouth. As a result, a staff member had to remove it so she could eat.

Because of these physical limitations, Violet slept and spent most of the day lying in a bed that was like a crib cage, with a vinyl mattress and rails around it. Usually, the rails stayed up while she slept or lay there, and only came down when we went to feed her or change the sheets.

Because of her digestive issues, her sheets often needed changing. Whenever this happened, we would remove the sheets from her bed and take off her clothes and get them into the laundry right away. Then, we would take her into a giant shower room where we would turn on the shower head to spray her down. The process was a little like washing a car, and it was inhumane when my coworker cleaned Violet up like she was cleaning an animal that had gotten dirty. As a result, I always tried to help Violet shower with more care, such as by talking to her and adjusting the shower head so the water was not too hot or too cold, and spraying her gently.

Additionally, I helped Violet with her bathing and personal care, which included drying her body, brushing her hair, and cleaning her mouth with lemon swabs and mouthwash. I put talcum powder on her butt, which she enjoyed, and around her neck where her helmet rubbed and reddened her skin. Then I had to put on her diaper and make sure that she was completely dry and that the diaper was not bunched or creased, since that would become uncomfortable for her later.

As I did these tasks, I had to remain upbeat and cheerful so that Violet would feel good about what she was doing, even though she had just made a huge smearing mess all over the floor. Though I often felt like vomiting on seeing such a mess, I did not want to let her know, since I did not want to upset her. As a result, Violet was normally extremely sweet and loving during this procedure, since she appreciated this personal connection.

In general, I was appalled at the way Violet was treated—locked in a hospital ward, living in a crib cage, and trapped in a helmet for more than twenty-two hours a day. I felt that if people had watched Violet more carefully after her first surgery, she would not have been required to live like that confined to her helmet and crib and with daily line-of-sight supervision. In turn, my awareness of Violet's treatment made me determined that people under my care would have a caregiver who thought that prevention and treatment were much better ways to deal with developmentally disabled patients than forcing them to live in a prison, as Violet did.

This is not to say that Violet was always treated badly. Occasionally I saw Ms. B in the lounge cuddling with Violet, whose helmet had been removed. During these times I would finish cleaning and remaking Violet's bed, so that Violet could enjoy that personal care and then return to clean, fresh sheets.

However, I also experienced several incidents during the 3-to-11 p.m. shift, when Violet lost control of her bowels and made a mess, which always required careful bathing afterward. At the time, other staff members got upset by what Violet did, as if she were doing it on purpose, although what happened was obviously not within her control. She was not responsible for her loose bowels and helmeted head, so it was up to the staff who assisted her to continue to treat her lovingly and not chastise or punish her for what she did. I would always try to remain upbeat, singing, laughing, and joking with her as I bathed her and cleaned her up.

At other times, when I thought of Violet engaging in destructive behaviors such as eating dangerous nonfood items, I felt truly angry because I had been trained to never leave substantial-risk people like Violet unsupervised. In her case, the staff should have employed line-of-sight supervision at all times—but they did not, which enabled her to engage in these destructive activities even while she was under their care. Even though this happened before I met her, I vowed this would never happen again while I was employed to watch over the residents of the ward.

My experience in caring for Violet led me to think about the importance of positive caregivers in my own life—for example, when *I* was ill and needed some personal care for myself. I found that it makes a difference when someone who is doing something for me has a truly caring attitude. If they do not, I hate what they are doing; if they do, I appreciate that they truly want to care for me. This personal reflection on caregiving helped me realize that I always want to make the people in my care feel they are truly being cared for.

In any case, for the first few weeks I worked at the New Jersey Institution, things were fine. I learned how to take blood pressure, changed dirty linens and diapers, and did other everyday tasks involved in caring for ill people. I enjoyed working with my co-workers, too. But my coworker Ms. B was a little hard to get to know, and I experienced the difficulties of working with a large employer and unionized workers at the beginning of my third week.

The problems began when we had a new admission to the institution. The man, who looked a little like Harry Belafonte, appeared a bit nervous as he walked onto the ward. Then, according to the usual procedures, we took him into a room to unpack his bags so we could look through everything and make sure there was nothing dangerous there. After that, we were supposed to strip him and complete a body chart to mark any scabs, scars, or other unusual physical characteristics. Then, we were supposed to dress him back up and show him to his room.

But after we got him naked, Ms. B punched him in the gut awfully hard and he doubled over. I looked on in shock, not knowing why she did this or what to do. Ms. B then explained, "This is how we teach the new admissions that we are in charge." I could not believe that a staff member could be allowed to do this, and I thought, *I've got to report this because it must be against the rules, since we don't physically abuse people who have mental disabilities and are helpless.*

However, before reporting anything, I talked to Ms. B about what happened, and she told me that what she did wouldn't matter to any supervisors because she was part of the union.

Then I spoke to our ward nurse about what Ms. B did, and the ward nurse simply said she was sorry this incident happened, and she would talk to Ms. B. But after she spoke to Ms. B, she told me that filing a report would be a lot of trouble for nothing. I was appalled to think that doing nothing was better than correcting a staff member who physically abused the hospital's patients. After that, I was determined not to allow those things where I worked, if I had the power to do so. But because I couldn't be everywhere at once, I also swore to do nothing but be kind to everyone.

Since I was a new hire in a low-level staff position there was not much that I could do. So I tried to get along as best I could, treating the patients with love and compassion. I tried to communicate with them however they were able to communicate, even if it was just by laughing with them or by touching and lifting their hand. It was as if I became their foster parent, ministering to their needs as I might to a child, and I fell in love with all of them, except for a few who became violent and attacked the staff by pulling their hair and spitting at or biting them.

Sometimes I was assigned to the other hospital wards. One was Ward B, which was comfortable for me because it was adjacent to Ward A, and I was familiar with the patients since I often spoke with the staff there. However, Wards C and D were quite different because they had much more medically fragile patients with greater needs. As a result, I had to be extremely careful about what I was doing, and be mindful of everything going on around me as I carried out my daily responsibilities.

My biggest responsibility was providing personal care, such as bathing the patients. Sometimes this proved quite difficult, because of a patient's developmental disabilities. For example, two patients had a rare hydrocephalus condition, in which the patients—both fifteen-year-olds—had normal bodies but unusually large heads. Their heads were so much larger than normal because they were full of excess fluid in the cavities deep within the brain, which resulted in a head four to five times the typical size. The reason for the increase is that the excess fluid from the spine expands the size of the ventricles, and this puts pressure on the brain, causing a bulging soft spot on the head along with any number of other disabilities. In the cases of these two patients, one person's head looked like a large, inflated balloon, and the other's was flat and squarely shaped.

Given their condition, I had to be especially careful in bathing these patients. The nurses trained me to carefully lift the head while they supported the body. Because we had to be so careful, we felt very tense as we slowly and cautiously bathed the patients. I felt especially anxious because I did not want to break their necks or drop them and do further damage. Then, too, I thought of them as very vulnerable babies, who felt very precious and needed respectful care.

As I cared for them, I came to learn much more about them and appreciate the abilities they did have. For example, it was hard for these patients to see, because of their limited mobility and damage to their occipital lobes, the area responsible for vision. However, they had great hearing, and they were fond of a few tunes with which the staff sometimes serenaded them. These mini concerts were also a time of great laughter. Sometimes I laughed so hard that I could not keep singing, and after we finished laughing, we would sing some more.

The patients sometimes reached out to me and other staff members with words and gestures of friendship. One young man was even a flirt, who grabbed my hand and held it as if he wanted me to be his girlfriend. After that, I just smiled at him and thought, *Even if you have a head five times too big for your body, and you are stuck laying down in a bed most of the time because it's hard to stand or sit, you can still be in the market for a girlfriend.*

Such experiences led me and the other workers on these wards to see the patients as deserving of dignity and gentle, efficient personal care. It was truly a memorable experience, and I was incredibly grateful for the wonderful coworkers I met when I was reassigned to Wards C and D.

After I had been working at the hospital for some time, I qualified for a scholarship to attend nursing school through an agreement between a nearby college and the New Jersey Institution. The agreement was that I would get my degree, and then come back and work at the Institution for four years. When I got this scholarship, I planned to become the ward RN and put a stop to any abuse of the patients.

I went to nursing school for eighteen months before I decided it wasn't for me. Although I liked being a caregiver and enjoyed learning about medical science, becoming a registered nurse did not inspire me, because so much of nursing involved tending to patients who were wounded and just seeing the blood and guts made me queasy. So I dropped out of college, and would only return several years later.

Becoming an Assistant In-House Manager for Developmentally Disabled Men

Two years later, in 1985, I started working as an assistant in-house manager at a group home in Hunterdon County for five developmentally disabled men. The house was run by the Hunterdon County ARC in Flemington, New Jersey. I lived in an apartment attached to the house the five men lived in. Everybody was professional and dedicated to their work.

My job was to be responsible for the care and integration of the men into their home and community. I was also responsible for supervising the staffing at the facility, instructing the staff members on what to do. But my main task was teaching the men some basic skills to help them adjust to living in the community. I also worked with the clients on creating their budgets, so they understood how to manage their finances, and I assisted them with grocery shopping. I gave them medication and documented the results. I helped organize and schedule workshops, too, to help train staff members and teach the clients new skills.

Additionally, I took the young men to and from the workshop where they spent their days. Then, back at the house, I made sure that we had all the needed groceries, and I went over receipts and various tasks assigned to me by the house manager. These included making careful reports of everything that I did during my shift and keeping them in a spiral notebook, our staff communication log.

Sometimes we took the men to dances, where they could dance with their friends. Since the men were extremely popular, they danced from the moment we arrived until the last song. Afterward, we would stop at the Dunkin' Donuts, and everybody sat at the counter and laughed and talked about the dance and who did what.

One of my favorite clients from that time was a handsome, charming man named Z, who loved Japanese culture and wore kimonos and high heels. However, he often obtained these shoes from unsuspecting staff members; this sometimes occurred when a person wore high heels to the house, but then took their shoes off and left them in the front door area and put on house shoes. Z would then slip away with one shoe, or the pair. Though he often put the shoes back, at other times those heels were never seen again.

Sometimes, in his affable charming way, he engaged in a friendly negotiation with the woman who had lost her heels. That occurred when the woman found her heels missing and became upset, wondering what happened to them. Then, Z would go over to her and let her know he had her beloved shoe in his bedroom tucked away in his kimono. He would then offer it back to her by producing the shoe and presenting it to her with a dramatic swoop of his right arm. Yet often his actions were so endearing that the women would leave wearing the house shoes instead.

I had to be careful that the door was locked between the home and my apartment, so that I would not find any high heels missing from my closet.

Besides Z's propensity for taking shoes, I soon learned many other things about him. Because he was so charming, I often forgot to be cross with him, though his personality was self-serving and manipulative. Yet his friendly demeanor hid some real tragedies in his background, as I learned from the other staff. They had gained this information from a briefing when Z first came to the center. As I found out, Z experienced such horrifying abuse while growing up that he had nearly died. A family member beat him, and his injuries were critical. As a result, he did not fully recover and became developmentally disabled.

The staff had few specific details, since Z could only remember a few points in his life before his disability. But his sad story haunted me and made me feel deeply sorry for him. His way of coping with the trauma he experienced was to be genuinely nice to people in order to mold them to like him and do things for him—a trait evident to all those who worked with him. Z was still so affected by his past trauma and current physical and mental disabilities, but I always told him to use his powers of persuasion for good.

I learned more about Z when I studied with the behavioral specialist who instructed the group home staff on how to deal with different patients when certain situations arose. For example, I learned from this specialist, and from my observations, that Z could use his "skill" for many purposes—for things as small as getting an extra cookie at dessert, or in more extreme scenarios, such as when he got into the home of a seventy-year-old woman who lived alone, after which the police arrested him for battery and put him in handcuffs because he had hit her.

As much as Z was charming, he could be dangerous—and he could potentially be dangerous for *me*, since I lived next to the center in a small apartment separated by only a hollow interior door. Conceivably, Z could get in and hurt me if I wasn't careful. With the help of the behavioral specialist, I learned and practiced scenarios with a behavioral therapy approach, which was designed to help Z make better decisions so he could have more choices and opportunities. I started with small choices, such as letting him stay up later to view his favorite television program if he got up on time the next day. Since he hated getting up in the morning, staying up late to enjoy his TV programs was an incentive and reinforcement to get up on time.

As a result, Z found it was worth it to control his decisions and make more positive choices because of the rewards he received for doing so, such as getting praise for his actions and more freedom to make choices. Due to these incentives to modify his behavior, he did well enough that he achieved several goals, one of which was visiting his sister and nephew. Those desired goals would have never been possible for Z without his successful behavioral therapy, which enabled him to control himself and make better choices.

Another patient I remember well was a man who was very enthusiastic about everything, though he was non-verbal, so he expressed his enthusiasm through his facial expressions and gestures. For example, he smiled a lot and clapped his hands enthusiastically, jumped up immediately to be the first to do something, made loud vocal sounds, paced about, and gave a quick kick, like a kangaroo, which hurt a lot if I was too close to him when it happened. Thus, outwardly, he seemed like a nice person, though I was never able to build a relationship with him—mainly because, in his enthusiasm, he frequently kicked out with high and extended kangaroo kicks, and he rarely missed his target. Since his kicks to the shins and legs really hurt, I did not like getting too close to him.

I also remember another patient, Mr. M, who became a good friend. He always looked very stern, but if one was kind and nice to him and his roommates, he was kind and gentle in return, so he was no trouble at all. On the other hand, if I or any other staff member had to be firm with him, he would become upset and be very mean to the staff. He would then tell his sister what we did when she came to visit him. She would go into his room, talk to him, and then tell us what Mr. M said about us.

In one instance, I made a mistake that landed me in hot water with Mr. M, who told his sister exactly what happened. But after his sister told me what he had said, she offered his diplomatic solution—just give him some extra applesauce, which I was extremely willing to do.

In another case that displeased Mr. M, I once lost my temper with another resident who had to get up at 5 a.m. to catch a 7 a.m. bus to his workshop. Unfortunately, this guy was incontinent, and each day he released what seemed like gallons of fluid in his bed, on the floor, on his clothing, and in his hair. So, he made the biggest mess with his sticky and smelling, dripping urine. Whenever this happened, I first had to get him out of his pajamas delicately and safely (he was also prone to seizures); then, while he showered, I had to strip his bed, start his laundry, and figure out how to mop everything up in order to keep him from re-soiling himself or tracking the mess into the rest of the house.

My mistake, in this case, was that Mr. M was standing nearby when I was cleaning up for this man, and he saw that I looked angry and frustrated in the way I frowned as I worked. Though I never yelled at the resident, Mr. M. could tell from the way that I grimaced and glared at him that I was angry and frustrated. Then, I made a rude, snippy comment to Mr. M, telling him something like, "Yes, go ahead and tell your sister that I'm pissed off about all this." So, of course, he told his sister, who confronted me with his complaint. After that, I wished I had not shared my anger and frustration with Mr. M, and since then I have practiced keeping anything I am upset about to myself. To this day I still remind myself, "You should keep anything negative to yourself. You should never let the patients see you sweat."

After eighteen months of this work, I had an enjoyable time and learned a lot, although I found it a little tiring working with people almost twenty-four hours a day; since I was living right there, the agency thought I could do the overnights for free.

But mostly, I liked my work for the New Jersey Institution and the Hunterdon ARC, and that again helped to reaffirm for me that I was right to decide on a career helping disabled people. It was like I was listening to a calling and following it on my career path.

Helping People Find Jobs in New Mexico

While my first jobs were in New Jersey, one of my group home coworkers planned to move to New Mexico and invited me to come along. My family had mostly moved to Florida, so I was the only one still in the New Jersey area besides my cousins and aunts. So, I decided, why not move? I had never been to New Mexico, though I had been on a cross-country trip in 1996 with my family; we traveled all the way to California and back, though mostly we followed a southern and then a northern route, so we bypassed New Mexico. But now I had an opportunity to go there.

I was also able to move since I had a part-time job at the Chicken Coop Lodge where I was a bartender, and I got a lot of helpful tips, especially during football games on Sunday. So, I was able to save up a lot of money. Oddly, though, when I told the people at the Chicken Coop where I was going to move, they thought I was going to Mexico. They did not even understand that there was a place called New Mexico, which I thought was funny.

Once I decided to move, I sold my car and almost everything I owned. A few days later, my friend and I put a box on top of her car, and we packed it to the gills. Then, we drove to New Mexico, where we first rented a room at the Cottonwood Court Motel. We made it as comfortable as possible while we read the rental section of the Santa Fe newspaper to find a more permanent place to stay.

I soon fell in love with my new home. I loved the warm weather, the vast open spaces, and the friendly, warm-hearted people I met, who made me feel very welcome.

Once I was there, I quickly found my first job working in a fast-food restaurant called the Burrito Company, where I worked behind the counter with the staff, filling orders and ringing up sales. I was the assistant manager, assigned to the evening shift. I worked with a bunch of high school kids, and I didn't make the best first impression. That is because, as I realized, in trying to be a manager I was using some of the techniques that I had learned working with people with developmental and other disabilities. But these methods did not go over very well with this group of kids. However, I soon adapted to having a more friendly, interactive approach, like I was a fellow employee, rather than treating the kids like patients I had to care for.

Soon my work and my relationships with the high school kids went more smoothly. The food there was delicious and wished I could cook it, but I never got the chance to do that. I also liked the company and the working conditions. The owner was a man who owned a couple of different businesses. I had a great manager named Mickey, who took me under his wing and helped me adapt my more controlling, East Coast management style to the more laid-back Santa Fe approach. This style worked even better for me because I could just tell the kids what to do and let them do their job without much supervision. I just had to check in to see if they had any questions about what to do. Plus, I could assign them the task of cleaning the restaurant, which made my life so much easier.

But as well as things were going, I knew the job was only temporary—just a way to earn some money and learn about the community while I looked for work in my chosen field. I found the perfect opportunity when I was hired at the Santa Maria El Mirador, which placed developmentally disabled individuals in group homes or apartments. My job was to help people find jobs, so that they could use their income to contribute to their rent.

Though I had never heard about such a profession, it proved to be a life-changing opportunity that eventually opened the door to what I am doing today—finding jobs for developmentally disabled people.

I found great inspiration from my first El Mirador supervisor, Bill Schiers. Bill had already completed a career in institutional management, specializing in mental and developmental disability. Bill was a great mentor to me, and he inspired me to continue my education. He also suggested papers, journals, and a short book I should read: *The History of Mental Retardation,* which I found invaluable and still have to this day. The book explained the various trends in the service and education of people with developmental disabilities, and it provided an overview of the historical medical treatments of and societal views toward these individuals, who, in western Europe and the United States, mostly lived in poverty as outcasts from the 1600s to the 1970s.

Bill also told me about the Supported Employment movement across the nation—a movement to help the developmentally disabled get training and find employment, though not much had been written about this at the time. Then, Bill enrolled me in two certificate courses at the University of New Mexico. I learned much and met particularly reliable professional contacts.

Yet while Bill encouraged supporting developmentally disabled individuals in the workplace, this was a time when supported employment was new and scary. Long-term El Mirador employees and the clients' family members alike expressed some resistance to my efforts to develop jobs for the individuals I worked with. They were afraid of my efforts, because these individuals had been segregated from the community in closed environments for so long, and, when they did work, they were generally only given very specific jobs, such as working in a greenhouse tending to plants. The employees and family members were concerned that these disabled individuals would not be successful when working jobs in the larger community. By contrast, I was eager to jump right in and place these people in jobs.

As a result, another supervisor, John DePaula, stepped in to educate my coworkers who were afraid of change. John had a kind way of encouragement, which helped to ease the fears of my coworkers. He also met with some of the family members to reassure them that their loved ones were ready and eager to take on these new opportunities in the community. His efforts helped to pave the way for greater acceptance of this push to help the developmentally disabled find more fulfilling jobs. But the most convincing proof would be seeing people actually become successful in these new jobs.

During this time in my life, I earned another big lesson on how to support people with disabilities. I learned to look to them to determine what they can do, rather than depending on reports and assessments which may assert that they cannot do something when they actually can. I realized this when I was coaching many of the clients that I worked with for the Special Olympics track and field events. Since no one was with me on the field except for the participants, I asked them what they wanted to do. Bobby said, "I like to run fast," so I put him in the quarter-mile dash. Yet two weeks later, when the staff in charge of Bobby arrived to see him practice, they informed me that he could *not* run fast, so I should not have placed him in the quarter-mile dash event.

"Why not?" I inquired, and explained that Bobby had a clear physician form, so there should not be anything barring him from competing.

They admitted that they had no reason to bar Bobby based on his medical record, but went on to say, "We do not know anything about how fast Bobby can run. But it is written in the book that he cannot run, and we always follow what it says in the book."

After that, I rechecked for any medical condition that would cause Bobby harm in running the quarter-mile dash. There was none, and Bobby was eager to race, so I gave him the go-ahead to do that—and he was successful in his race.

This experience with Bobby was a big lesson for me since it showed me the importance of looking to the individual to see what they can and want to do. Thus, I always try to look at the abilities and desires of my clients first, rather than going by some guidebook that claims a developmentally disabled person cannot do something. Oftentimes they can, if given the chance to try. Accordingly, I found that putting the individual's desires and abilities first and asking them what they want to do is a successful way to build a positive relationship, and is the best way to coach them for success.

Meanwhile, as I continued to work at the Santa Maria El Mirador, I took courses at the University of New Mexico. Together, my experience at El Mirador and my education at the university led me to find a new way of reaching out to people to help them find jobs.

The usual approach to job recruiting is to sit in an office and spend most of the time on the phone talking to potential employers and employees seeking work. Then, one would look for matches between the jobs offered and the experience of the prospective employees.

I started going out in the community, mainly to places in the restaurant and grocery industries, like Pizza Hut and Homeland Grocery Store. When I found job openings, I offered them to the people who needed employment opportunities. This approach turned out to be very successful; in fact, I know that of one of the men I helped to place in a job is still working at the same company after many decades.

In developing this placement approach, I put in lots and lots of legwork, calling on businesses repeatedly. Though the doors were sometimes shut when I first called on a company, my persistence paid off. I found that it often took three visits to a business before the owners or managers felt comfortable listening to my pitch about my clients looking for a job. It was common for them to initially express some resistance, because they had not worked with developmentally disabled employees before and did not trust them to do the job.

However, I was able to explain the advantages of giving these employees a chance. As I told them, "The national ARC has a wonderful grant program that reimburses employers the salary of an employee hired through a supported employment placement. The ARC will pay back the wages after the employee has met certain milestones for remaining on the job." Once I had explained how this reimbursement program worked, it proved to be a big enticement for many employers, especially the rural employers of Espanola and Alcalde, New Mexico. Once an employer hired a developmentally disabled employee, they quickly realized that the arrangement proved to be a good fit. No one ever had to leave an employer after the reimbursement ran out. Instead, the employees remained on the job.

Getting a BA in Management and Working in a New Job

I entered the University of Phoenix to finish my Bachelor of Arts in Management. I attended on line and in person university, but most of the learning was done online and in study groups.

Around the time I obtained my diploma, a new job in marketing opened at Santa Maria El Mirador and I applied for the position. I didn't get it, but I felt I did not get a fair shot at the job because I was young. I also did not feel they made a desirable choice for the new marketing director; the person did not strike me as a good fit, mainly because he was uncomfortable around our developmentally disabled clients and acted condescending to them, despite the fact that our work was all about helping them. Thus, this was not a person I respected or trusted.

Following this episode, I decided it was time to look at other employers. I found a job opening at a national for-profit company called ResCare, which had its main New Mexico office in Albuquerque. The company hired me to develop business in northern and eastern New Mexico, which included Santa Fe, Espanola, Clovis, Roswell, and all the towns in between. I grew the company in my areas and focused on providing home-based services and some vocational services. I loved the work and the company. I was successful and believed that the job was a great match for me at that time in my life.

One of the clients I worked with had a dual diagnosis, meaning she had both mental health and developmental issues. Yet despite her difficulties, she was resourceful and always eagerly told me about her latest new ideas, such as her ability to find lost coins everywhere. Because of this ability, she could go out for a walk and return with the pockets of her Levi's bulging with change, so that it looked like her legs had extra big muscles. She made a practice of carrying her large coin collection around with her, which made her smell like copper and dirt; she was never without them, except for the occasional times that she would cash them in for paper money, or when I arranged for her to go on job interviews.

I had to divest her of her coins for these interviews, since my job was to help her to get neat, clean, and presentable to the community, especially when she went to interview for a job. She also produced her own creative way of preparing for these interviews, which she described to me one day when she arrived for our meeting in my office.

"Sweetie, I figured it out," she told me. "I went to the car wash, and I had a shower and washed my clothes at the same time."

I was surprised at her unusual clean-up method, and though I admired her creativity, I had to tell her that this approach could not be a permanent option. As I explained to her, it would soon be too cold to make outdoor car washes her routine for doing her laundry and bathing. After she realized that was indeed the case, she used the showers and sinks at the center to wash herself and her clothes.

Sexuality

Let me begin this section with an excerpt by my friend and mentor Judy Myers a Nationally recognized leader in the field of sexuality and intellectual, developmental disabilities and autism has written this section to educate us.

I am starting this discussion of sexuality for individuals with Intellectual Disabilities/Developmental Disabilities (ID/DD) with my favorite quote from Dr. Jacqueline Forest.

"Parents still hold on to the false hope that if they don't mention sex, and the child doesn't hear about sex, somehow the child won't have any idea that sex even exists!"

This hope is indeed false in so many ways. Some parents refer to children with ID/DD as "forever children," but the fact is they *do* go through adolescence just like everyone else. The question is, are parents and/or caregivers prepared for these changes, and able to explain them? Individuals with ID/DD need simple, factual information in order for them to make good decisions. We do these individuals a disservice if we do not provide this guidance; in the worst case, without the benefit of sex education they can even become victims of abuse and sexual violence.

The primary reason I address this is because so often when caregivers support folks with ID/DD, the individual has little if any knowledge concerning sex. Caregivers need to know how to ask questions and be prepared with appropriate answers to questions asked, whether it's about holding hands, having a boyfriend or girlfriend, kissing, dating, and, yes, masturbation.

Everyone absorbs information in snippets, not "the talk" all in one session. Your responsibility is to answer only what is asked. If asked, "Can my friend and I hold hands?", an appropriate answer might be, "As long as it's okay with both of you, then yes." You don't need to feel like you have to launch into a talk on masturbation.

We keep learning our whole lives, one lesson at a time. Think about your math experience in first grade. Were you presented with all math at once, never to have another math class again? Though some may *wish* they never had another math class, the reality is that you had math every year, and learned a little more each time—just what was appropriate for your age and maturity. The same goes for sexuality; the lessons should change as a person gains information and life experiences.

Sexuality is part of who we are. It is biological, like eating, sleeping, making friends, breathing, laughing, feeling sad, and so on. It is part of our senses—seeing, hearing, smelling, and touching. It is an individual choice—some chose to not have sex, while others experience it often. We are all alike but different.

I once had an individual we were supporting ask to speak to me in private. When we went to my office, the question he asked was, "Can I have sex?" My response was, "Tell me a little bit more."

He went on to say, "I want to have lunch with a girl." To him, that was sex! I was able to give him some appropriate advice in the moment; later, he attended one of my classes on THE TALK.

Always remember to give correct and appropriate information based on an individual's questions and level of understanding. Should someone ask questions you are uncomfortable answering, refer them to someone else. "I'm not sure I can answer that, let's go talk to Mr./ Ms. So-and-so."

If you feel that someone with ID/DD would benefit from learning in a more formal setting, I suggest you coordinate with a professional in the field of sexuality to give classes that both caregivers and the individuals in their care can attend. It's important that caregivers also are present because some individuals may have questions that they do not want to ask in the classroom. This is often because they are not yet comfortable with the instructor, or even with the other participants—but they'll know that they can later ask you, the caregiver.

Stephan Bechtel has a good approach to sexuality: "Don't be embarrassed. Always ask questions. Call the body parts by the correct name (not some slang or made-up name). Know your own sexual values. Saying nothing is saying something."

I also have two references that might be helpful. IntellectAbility is a website where you can keep up with the most current trends in ID/DD.

The second is a presenter, the parent of a child with ID/DD and the author of four books on ID/DD, including one on sexuality. Look her up on the Web.

Learn to embrace asking questions of the individuals you support, and answering their questions honestly; remember, they ask you because they trust you.

Until this point in my career, most of the sexuality I witnessed in the course of working with my clients had been what would be termed "inappropriate" behavior—things like the high heel thief, individuals masturbating in public, and other behaviors.

But the truth is, people are people and have the same desires, no matter what. To be honest with you, I am a prude in this arena. I turn my head to preserve my clients' privacy, and I abhor the violent portrayal of sex illustrated on screens and in print. However, as the quote at the beginning of this section suggests, not thinking about sex is not an effective means of preventing its existence. And there have been times in my career when I've encountered sexuality head-on, in various ways.

In one case, I was working with a new client, Katie. She and her husband Rick both had cerebral palsy. Katie needed total physical assistance, while Rick was independent and worked outside the home in a very well-paid position. My job primarily involved working with Katie during the day, when Rick was at work. Despite needing physical assistance, Katie was independent otherwise; I and other staff would help her get up, dressed, and settled in her power chair for the day.

One day Rick had a meeting with me. He said that he and Katie wanted to have sexual relations in their marriage bed, but that he could not manage both of their physical positions by himself. Could I help?

"Oh my gosh," I said, getting red and embarrassed, "you mean me, Rick? You want me to help Katie get ready to be intimate with you?"

"Yes, that is correct," Rick said. "Of course, you will not be in the room when the time comes, Lisa."

"Of course—I'm sure I will not be in the *house*, Rick." *Man,* I thought when the meeting was over, *what do I do? How do I even do this? Am I even* supposed *to do this?*

My case manager Caroline was a great mentor for me here. She came over and we both discussed the situation with Katie privately. Katie was not that into it, but she knew that this was part of being married and really loved Rick and was willing. So, we decided how we were going to go about the assistance.

Katie had a great attitude and was used to staff people seeing her naked for personal care. We got her bathed and wearing a pretty negligee, did her hair, and placed her in the bed the way she and Rick thought would work best for them. We left the room. Rick went in. As predicted, I left the house at once.

Rick called me three hours later and said Katie was fine and that I did not need to help her anymore that evening. In the morning, Katie was beaming and super happy about her experience with her husband.

This process became easier over time, and eventually just became part of the job duties. They also got more independent with it. Imagine being married and having to plan your sexual activity with direct care aid; it was hard for me, and I know it was for them, too. But we did our part to help them be happy.

Two other occurrences in Santa Fe involved sexual incidents, both involving men. Both men had cerebral palsy. One used a chair and required 100 percent physical assistance. His family had devised a board with the letters of the alphabet and a pointer that could be affixed to his head, allowing him to spell out words one letter at a time to communicate. Arduous, but it worked. This guy and I worked together for a long time, and it got to the point that I could practically speak for him; I could say what I thought he meant, and he would agree if I was right and disagree if not.

Once we had been working together for a while, he told me that the staff member who worked with him on weekends engaged in sexual activity with him. He was upset because he initially agreed to do it, but he now wanted it to stop. I explained to him that it is not consensual when a person who is paid and entrusted to care for someone else engages in sexual activity with them. We helped him through counseling to understand that he was a victim. During the investigation that followed, it turned out that this staff person had been perpetrating sexual abuse not only on my client but on little girls in New Mexico and the panhandle of Oklahoma as well. He was prosecuted, and my client spelled out the information to the DA one letter at a time; his testimony helped to put the man in jail.

The third case had to do with a man who was living inde-pendently. He would walk the streets at night, doing things to get attention; based on his behavior, the attention he got was usually negative. He would lie down in puddles and get soaking wet in the freezing cold. Someone would call an ambulance, and they would call me. I would go get him and take him home. I never knew why he was doing this sort of thing, and he could never explain it. Was he lonely and needing a roommate? No, he liked his independence. It remained a mystery.

One night it was cold, and snow and ice covered the street and sidewalks. I had been called to the hospital to meet him after another of these incidents. When I was dropping him at home, he was clearly very aggravated—beyond anything I had seen from him before. He suddenly lunged at me. Though I hate to say it, the truth is that, since he had physically attacked me before, I wasn't surprised but simply shifted to protecting myself.

This guy was pure muscle, faster and stronger than me. I tried to defend myself, but moving away was hard on the ice. I discovered that I could get him off balance when he lunged at me. He fell, and had a challenging time getting up. He was still really aggravated, and it looked like he was swimming at me through the ice and snow. He grabbed my leg and bit me; even though I had jeans and my Dan Post boots on, he bit me so hard he broke the skin through my jeans and boots. Wow. This was serious, and I needed help.

Eventually others were able to intervene, and he calmed down. We were able to get a sign language expert to translate his version of ASL. It turned out that the neighbor in the adjoining apartment was sexually abusing him, which is why he kept leaving his safe, warm home on dark, cold nights. He was asking for help in the only way he knew how.

That neighbor was also prosecuted, and it again turned out that this man had abused other victims; a number of them testified against him. We found my client a roommate and a live-in staff person for him. He was happy and felt safe, and he did not physically attack people anymore after that.

These incidents were just a few points that occurred during the period of my career I spent in New Mexico. I learned a lot in this time; however, as much as I enjoyed my work, I eventually realized that it was time to move on. In my personal life, I was raising my nephew, since his father had moved to Oklahoma City. I figured it would be good for the boy to be closer to his dad, so I decided to look for jobs in Oklahoma.

I found an ideal job when an opening with ResCare Oklahoma became available—and I was ultimately hired to be the State Director. This meant a major career boost, since the program was huge and there would be 500 employees and 130 clients under my care.

One of the reasons I got my job is because of what happened at the Hissom Memorial Center, which had originally been built to serve individuals with developmental disabilities in the Tulsa area. It was closed due to a lawsuit in 1994. So let me describe what happened there, and how it led to my working at ResCare.

CHAPTER 2

What Happened At The
Hissom Memorial Center

At one time, there was great hope for the Hissom Memorial Center. It was the one state-sponsored center for individuals with developmental disabilities in the area of Tulsa, Oklahoma. It opened on March 5, 1964, with great fanfare.

The Hissom Memorial Center

In the 1950s, before the Hissom Memorial Center was built, the two schools that served as mental health facilities in Oklahoma were the Enid and Paul's Valley State Schools. Because these schools were overcrowded, Governors Raymond Barry and J. Howard Edmondson decided to start a project to build a new school with modern ideas. The construction of this new school began in 1961 on land donated by Mr. Wiley G. Hissom and local hobby cattle farmers in the area.

It took around five years to complete the Center, which was named after its major donor. It had twenty-four buildings on eighty-five acres and was able to treat up to 1,200 patients by providing diagnostic treatment, rehabilitation, training, outpatient services, and research.

Once the Center was completed, students could enroll by following a special procedure, which began with diagnostics and evaluation. Once accepted, students had a chance to learn and enjoy the swimming pool, gymnasium, educational field trips, and other activities, for a maximum fee of $75 a month, although there were some discounted and free scholarships for students of limited economic means.

The Center received no money from the state, because state officials believed that people with disabilities were troublesome to their families and other children; such people believed they belonged in institutions, rather than going to a center that was in the community and was dedicated to training and support.

Yet even though it received no support from the state, the Center continued to thrive from the monthly fees from students and some private donations. As a result, the Center served its students successfully for two decades, until 1985. That is when a nurse and some parents of students who attended the school started a lawsuit against the Center, saying that it was a dangerous place to live.

The Lawsuit Against the Hissom Memorial Center

The lawsuit against the Hissom Memorial Center began after Ms. MaryAnn Duncan sought help with raising her two foster kids, who had disabilities. She was unable to care for them herself because of some personal hardships.

Thus, Duncan enrolled her kids in the Center. They lived there for three weeks before they were allowed to come home for a visit. But when they returned home, Duncan noticed that their clothes were too big, and their pants were held up by rope. She also saw that one boy had a broken tooth and a fungal infection on his scalp. She was especially concerned when the kids refused to go back to Hissom at the end of their short stay at home.

While Duncan was able to convince the two kids to return to Hissom, soon afterward, on a cold wintry day, she received a call saying that her kids had gotten sick. When she arrived to take them home, she noticed that one boy's face and shoulder were burned, because he had been lying in his vomit for several days.

Duncan was appalled that her kids faced such conditions, and she spoke to some other parents about the experiences of their kids. As a result, Duncan and the parents realized that the treatment provided at Hissom was substandard, and the Center needed to change its practices immediately.

Among other things, they began to research lawsuits in other states in the country, and with the help of the Public Interest Law Center of Philadelphia, they launched a lawsuit against the state of Oklahoma. The lawsuit requested that Hissom fix their terrible treatment methods for the kids, as well as provide compensation for their failings.

But this was just the beginning, as the lawsuit revealed other evidence of abuse. For example, research for the lawsuit indicated that Herbito Martinez, one of the doctors working with the center, was practicing as a doctor using fake credentials. This was a criminal matter, and he was convicted and sentenced to two and a half years in prison. Additionally, after the lawsuit was filed, the federal judge trying the case discovered that two men were abusing the children in the facility; they were subsequently charged and convicted.

As a result of the lawsuit and the criminal charges against some of the men associated with the Center, U.S. District Judge James Ellison decided that the facility should be closed. He ordered the closure of the Center on July 24, 1987.

However, it took another seven years of legal procedures for Hissom to finally close. Initially, Duncan and other parents of kids at the Center were delighted with the ruling, since they felt their kids could now live a peaceful and independent life without being hampered by institutional restrictions, and without suffering abusive or substandard care.

But as is often the case in civil litigation, the Center filed an appeal, which wended its way through the courts and led, in 1988, to the state of Oklahoma appealing Ellison's original ruling to the 10th Circuit Court of Appeals, which extended the deadline for closing the facility and moving its patients to the community.

Finally, on May 4, 1994—the ninth anniversary of the lawsuit—the Hissom Memorial Center was officially closed.

What the Lawsuit Helped Teach about Individuals with Developmental Disabilities

While the lawsuit was all about closing and penalizing the Center for its harmful acts against its patients, the proceedings also helped to illuminate some of the key things that developmentally disabled individuals need and want. As Jordan Didier, an agency spokesperson put it, "From the lawsuit, we have learned a lot of things that prove that individuals with developmental disabilities want the same things that you and I want. They want to work independently, live independently, and be able to go to the movies with their friends. Every one of them wakes up every day and makes a conscious decision that they will not be what everyone thinks they should be."

In other words, apart from any legal decisions and criminal convictions resulting from the lawsuit, the litigation focused more attention on the needs and abilities of the developmentally disabled. This shift in focus provided the groundwork for the opening of ResCare, and the work that I was then able to do at the agency.

CHAPTER 3

Working For A Statewide Branch Of A National Corporation In Oklahoma

Initially, I had been up against four other applicants for the director job at ResCare; though I was thrilled to get the job, I hoped I could do it since it involved significant managerial responsibilities. Fortunately, I had already worked at ResCare New Mexico with the person who would be my new supervisor, so I did know someone who could help me. I would also be working alongside professional, well-trained staff, who were experienced in working with people with developmental disabilities. Still, the position represented a big leap for me.

Don't Blow Your First Impression

Once I started on the job, one of the first things I wanted to make clear to my staff was that we were working *together* to take care of the clients in our care. I explained that though I was the boss, I could not do anything alone. I said that I while had experience in the field, I could not claim to know everything. I told them, "You are all part of my team, and I have no choice but to trust you and your work representing ResCare Oklahoma. As members of the team, I will be on your side. We are in this together. All I ask is that you be honest with me, whatever the situation."

Then, I told my new team a story about myself. I explained to them what I learned on my first day of kindergarten. "Before arriving at school, my mother told me, 'I am like a mother lion protecting her cubs. Going to school is going to be different from what you are used to. There will be times when there is trouble, and you are involved. If that happens, tell me the truth about what went on. Even if you are in the wrong, we can get through it. Do not lie to me, because if you do, I cannot protect you—and I am *supposed* to protect you. But if you lie to me, I will not be able to trust you.'"

As I explained to my team, I was extremely glad to have had this advice from my mother in my first year of school, because I frequently found myself explaining and apologizing throughout my primary school years. Thus, just as my mother expected me to be honest with her, that is what I expected of my staff.

As a young manager, I wanted to use this initial meeting with my staff to make sure my team knew what *I* was willing to do, and what I expected *them* to do. I also wanted them to know I did not want to be the kind of executive director who sat in the office and never dealt with the customers. Also, I felt if the staff knew I came from a direct care position and built my way up, they would respect my opinions and direction better.

Naturally, things were not smooth with my new management team. One of them felt that she deserved the promotion to Director. Sabotage was in the air. Rumors spread about my past faux pas, both real and imagined. That employee who felt she'd been passed over suddenly had an "attitude" problem. On several occasions, she publicly resorted to negative behavior and acted sullen with official visitors and coworkers. *Yikes, not another Burrito Company situation*, I thought to myself.

But thanks to my relationship with Sybil, my manager, disaster was averted. I could talk things over with her openly and receive her experienced mentorship. At this time I honestly can't remember how we handled the situation, but I do know that I was much calmer and more confident thanks to her advice. Eventually, the troublesome person resigned. The gal that replaced her had similar thoughts and values as myself regarding vocational services for the people to whom we provided services. She was full of new ideas, a go-getter and self-starter who produced incredible job opportunities that ended in success for our customers.

This situation helped me realize and understand the struggles involved in managing direct reports. While it wasn't hard to determine this particular person's issue, it did make me worry about the rest of the team. Could they, too, be harboring resentments? Could I ever be successful in connecting with them and building productive relationships? But I realized that I shouldn't jump to conclusions; instead, I should observe, invite them in, support them, and stick to the workplace culture I was building—and then I'd see what they were made of, and whether or not they were working WITH me.

My team did not get to choose who was going to be their boss. But the big thing I learned is that they do get to decide whether they want *you* as their boss. If they have the strengths you need, and fit with the culture you're trying to build, and want to be part of the team, then great. If not, help them find a better fit. The more mutual this decision is, the better. Sometimes I had to ask people to leave; many other times, people chose on their own to go in a new direction. More times than I can count, former employees would thank me for helping them pursue a new path, because they wound up finding what worked best for them. Don't get me wrong I indeed made many mistakes—but always learned as I grew.

My recent experience as a job developer helped me see how best to use the talent on my staff. Interestingly, a person employed as a residential program manager was better suited to work in an accountant position—and, with support from the corporate office, it worked perfectly. After a long career in accounting, this person is now working as the CEO of a nonprofit developmental disabilities provider.

Later, I took some time to learn about the many different management styles, and the one that impressed me most was the Disney management style. This approach tells us that the people we serve are guests, and the staff people are cast members. I love this analogy because it implies that we are playing a role to be the best worker we can be. Then, too, I wanted to make working on the job fun.

The Biggest Job Ever

Working with ResCare as the State Director proved to be a wonderful opportunity, since it allowed me to add extensive management experience to my background in caring for developmentally disabled patients. It was also my first experience working for a large national company with offices in different states, since ResCare is a for-profit, statewide, national company traded on the New York Stock Exchange.

As the State Director, I was responsible for the company's day-to-day operations and oversaw all personnel and accounting functions. I managed all the company's programs, which included supported living, nursing, vocational services, and community waivers. These waivers contributed to the living expenses of developmentally disabled individuals, since they qualify for institutional care. As such, they can live in an intermediate care facility, like the New Jersey Institution, or they can live directly in the community through a community waiver, which allows them to receive services where they live rather than in an institutional setting. They can choose which type of living arrangement they prefer. Additionally, I developed and managed the company's budgets, and I reported to the Corporate Office in Louisville, Kentucky.

While I was at ResCare, I served in its national Quality Assurance Program, which involved traveling to different states to review the quality of services. I also learned about several national accreditation organizations that survey agencies for the different services they provide, and, about the state and federal government programs that provide funding to control service quality by developing and implementing quality assurance surveys.

One accreditation organization I dealt with regularly was the Commission on the Accreditation of Rehabilitation Facilities, or CARF, which was responsible for checking that our services provided quality care. I liked the CARF process because it allowed me to learn from the surveyors and share my suggestions about what the Commission was doing.

Eventually, I volunteered to be on the national quality assurance team, which meant surveying other businesses that were part of the ResCare corporation in order to ensure that they were following the ResCare Quality Way. This was a care model that I was proud to work with because it placed a high value on the rights of the clients and treated them with respect and dignity; it did not treat them as if they were of less value because of their developmental disability.

As a member of the national quality team, I visited programs in Texas, Colorado, Louisiana, and Oregon to make sure they were adhering to the high quality standards for caring for the disabled. This review additionally helped me learn about the various programs and rates in different states; this provided insights into what worked best, so that these best practices could then be shared with the managers of the programs in all the states. I found it especially enlightening to compare these programs in different states because they were often vastly different.

For example, in the Oklahoma programs, each person either has their own home or lives in a home with other disabled roommates. By contrast, the Colorado programs provide for adult foster homes, called host homes, and the persons receiving services live in these homes. Then, too, the services provided by these programs vary from state to state in the way they teach, train, and support their developmentally disabled clients.

The quality and delivery of care were particularly important to me, but I recognized that quality service could be provided successfully in different ways. Along with my concern with providing diligent care, as a manager I made sure that ResCare met stringent profit margins while providing a competitive wage to the direct support staff who worked for us. In turn, having this competitive wage made the company an attractive place to work for staff members who were best qualified to provide excellent service.

Working for ResCare was both stressful and inspiring because it was the biggest job I ever held. One advantage was that I got to go to a lot of big meetings and national conferences. I also became part of the American Network of Community Options and Resources (ANCOR), and I joined the board of directors as a state representative from Oklahoma. At the time, it was exciting, fun, and a great opportunity to learn about the field—and later, what I gained from participating in these national activities helped me develop the idea of creating my own agency.

Working for State Public Policy Changes

Some of the most inspiring work I did involved the time I spent advocating for public policy changes at the state level. In Oklahoma, there was one statewide provider association that met with state officials to share and receive information. Unfortunately, it was classified as an educational non-profit; therefore it could not become involved with legislation, especially with lobbyists.

In order to get involved in state politics affecting our programs, my agency, ResCare, and six of the state's other largest providers formed a coalition to explore our options. We called it ONCOR—Oklahoma Network of Community Options and Resources. This was during the time that I was serving as the Oklahoma representative on the board of ANCOR, the American Network of Community Options and Resources. ANCOR had no problem with our choice of name and sent their support for our efforts.

One of the first lobbyists we connected with was Clem McSpadden, a legislative lobbyist in Oklahoma. During our first interview he told me, "I'm the Walmart of lobbyists," by which he meant that he was both immensely popular and charged the lowest prices. I soon discovered that his claim was true when I looked at the credentials and prices of other lobbyists to represent our coalition. Clem not only had the best price, but he had an awesome reputation on both sides of the political aisle.

ONCOR hired Clem because of his stellar reputation and political connections over his career spent as a rodeo announcer and politician. Clem was a member of the Democratic Party and served as the U.S. Representative from Oklahoma's 2nd Congressional District from 1973 to 1975. Before then, he was a member of the Oklahoma State Senate between 1954 and 1972. He also discovered the remarkably successful country singer, Reba McIntyre, and helped her get noticed by hiring her to sing the national anthem at rodeos; since then, they remained close.

Policymakers in state government did not know what service providers experienced in seeking to satisfy new, burdensome, and often expensive regulation. They did not realize this because they did not understand the effects of the legislation they passed on the agencies and organizations seeking to help the disabled.

Accordingly, with help from McSpadden, we began setting up face-to-face meetings with the Director of the Oklahoma Department of Human Services and the Developmental Disability Services (DDS) department heads. Our goal was to educate them about what kind of programs and legislation was needed to provide the appropriate services for disabled individuals. These first meetings were tense; members were leery of the state's motives and trustworthiness, and vice versa. It was a little tricky to navigate between the two state agencies and the members of ONCOR. Fortunately, ONCOR's seasoned professional provider agency directors forged ahead and developed effective dialogue between ONCOR members and the department officials who made policy.

This dialogue eventually led to our first agreement—the DDS was to share proposed policy changes with us and consider our input in making further changes. This agreement was extremely important, since it was very helpful for providers to know about changes. ONCOR members were adamant that the agreement include self-advocates and families, so that they could stay informed about policy changes and provide input. This way, before any changes were implemented, meetings were arranged for DDS and the service providers, self-advocates, and families to discuss the effects of the proposed policy to all the people involved. It opened a dialogue that otherwise would not have happened. The Oklahoma Department of Human Services Director, Howard Hendrick, was incredibly open to listening, providing information, and assisting families affected by his department. Additionally, DDS Director James Nicholson supported providers and service recipients, while always maintaining political correctness. I admired and enjoyed working with both Director Nicholson as well as DDS Communications Director Sheree Powell.

Clem and his son Bart, who was also a lobbyist, helped us become successful in our lobbying efforts, and I learned a great deal about the political process and getting bills passed. Among other things, Bart and his then-business partner Jami Longacre helped me develop a training course to teach people how to approach legislators and lobby for the issues they are passionate about. Such training was very necessary because most people are afraid of legislators; they think they are so powerful that it's not possible to even talk to them.

To make it easier for people to become advocates, we conducted several sessions around the state to help parents and self-advocates learn their rights and how to exercise them by talking to their elected officials. We practiced "elevator speeches," in which the students pretended they were on an elevator with the head of the finance committee or some other influential official. The students would then practice what they would say to encourage the official to support a certain piece of legislation by the time the elevator ride ended.

Once the students perfected their elevator speeches, the course taught them to be ready for any opportunity that might arise. As the course materials advised them, "Do not hesitate. Introduce yourself. Tell the person coming onto the elevator of your or your child's needs before the doors open to let him off."

The course was so successful that we signed up participants from all over Oklahoma, and legislators came to know the issues that the course's participants raised with them for many years. We even dubbed the students who took the course "The Capital Commandos," because they were so well trained and effective.

To build momentum, we met once a month with people from all over the state at local community colleges. The Commandos just had to make a few phone calls, and they had access to meeting rooms with video networking systems where we could livestream meetings—and this at a time when they were uncommon in the early 2000s. The students loved these digital meetings, and they proved to be a wonderful way to get parents and self-advocates activated, since they could stay in their towns and meet their neighbors who had the same mission. The Capital Commandos helped our success in lobbying for change and rate increases under McSpadden's direction.

As a result of these activities, I became quite attached to Clem and Bart and made many lifetime friends in the halls of the Oklahoma state capital. Though both Bart and Clem are now deceased, I often think about how much I learned from them, especially from Clem's life lessons, which he shared through his powerful storytelling. Up until he died of cancer on July 7, 2008, Clem was an inspiration for providing care, since he was passionate about caring for the individuals for whom we were lobbying.

Going into the political arena, our goals were to accomplish public policy change, create open communication with policymakers, support our professional staff by providing professional wages, and increase reimbursement rates—all in an effort to provide better care for the Oklahomans receiving our services. We lobbied for fiscal relief, because back then, in the late 1990s and early 2000s, we were struggling for money to provide wages for our staff. Of course, this is a struggle that still continues to this day.

Due to our efforts, we created partnerships with parents, policymakers, and, most importantly, self-advocates. Though I was not involved in creating these self-advocacy groups, I was impressed and inspired by them, and I wanted to help them gain more leverage to obtain government support and funding for their efforts. One exciting opportunity presented itself to self-advocates in Oklahoma in 2011. The Commissioner of the Federal Administration on Developmental Disabilities, Sharon Lewis, invited these Oklahoma self-advocates to a regional self-advocacy summit. The summit partners attending included six groups involved in assisting the disabled. They were: Oklahoma People First (OPF); Self-Advocates Becoming Empowered (SABE); the National Youth Leadership Forum (YLF); the Center for Learning and Leadership (CLL); the Developmental Disabilities Council of Oklahoma (DDCO); and the Oklahoma Disability Law Center (ODLC). The Oklahoma Department of Human Services, Developmental Disabilities Services (OKDHS/DDS), also attended.

The advocates who attended the summit were very inspired and wanted to share their enthusiasm to effect change not only among themselves but with all their peers with developmental disabilities. For example, the members of OPF asked their partners, "**Teach us to do it ourselves.**" The voices and actions of those partners contributed to the development and passage of voting access laws and improved accessibility. They also helped to develop inclusion provisions that provide the developmentally disabled with a better opportunity to vote. Thus, this group effectively got things changed and gained wide respect throughout the community of the disabled and their advocates.

Their view is shared by every agency in Oklahoma helping the disabled; as a result, they have included self-advocates in their efforts to reach out to legislators and promote certain changes in the law and policies. Oklahoma has strong self-advocacy networks that receive support from many state and private funders.

OPF additionally inspired other advocacy groups with their mantra, "**Nothing about us without us.**" What this means is that the developmentally disabled community does not want outsiders deciding what is best for them; rather, the disabled and their advocates want to be intimately involved in the process of self-determination by members of their community. This mantra got me thinking about how my agency and ONCOR members should 100% be involved in advocacy for ourselves, sharing our success stories and continued needs with legislators and our community. The people receiving much-needed HTS and job coaching services need their neighbors to be supportive and to help in assisting the developmentally disabled more freely access their communities.

Money: Let's Talk About Funding

Funding is what state and federal governments pay contract providers to do their work. Providers are given whatever rate is established by the funder. We cannot raise prices for our services; they are set, and it takes a lot of effort to change them. It was long overdue for Oklahoma DDS providers to heavily lobby to increase the funding for direct care services contracted with OKDHS/DDS. Here is the story of how funding for our services changed from the time I arrived to work in Oklahoma through the time when our political advocacy began. The information and facts below come from a 2001 ONCOR report to the Oklahoma Senate and House Human Services Subcommittee on Appropriations.

OKDHS/DDS has many services with corresponding reimbursement rates. Today we are exploring the most used service, Habilitation Training Specialist (HTS).

A Developmentally Disabled Oklahoman who needs services goes through the following steps:

1. Application to DDSD.
2. DDSD determines eligibility, type, and level of service needed.
3. Person is placed on the DDSD waiting list.
4. When funding for services is available the person is notified of eligibility.
5. DDSD Case Managers provide Consumers and their Parents/Guardians with a list of available providers.
6. Consumers interview potential agencies and then choose the provider who can best meet their needs.
7. The Interdisciplinary team meets and determines the level of service to be provided by Residential, Vocational, Therapy, and Behavioral Providers.

8. The Provider Agency assigns a Program Coordinator, who in turn works closely with the Consumer and Family to hire and train the HTS Staff.

Challenges face service provider agencies, which is why we were and continue to ask for an increase in funding.

- Recruitment, training, and retaining qualified direct support staff continues to be a struggle with turnover up to 66% at times.
- Population issues in the future mean even fewer people will become HTS. Baby boomers, who in 2030 will be aged 66 to 84, will number sixty-one million people. 1 in 5 people will be of retirement age. The working population will be less than the older population. We knew in 2003 that longer life spans, the high number of baby boomers, and the smaller size of subsequent generations would cause there to be fewer caregivers in the future. We all expect to get old, so it is everyone, not just the developmentally disabled, who will need human caregivers.

The 1994 HTS rate was set at $12 an hour. Due to the Oklahoma budget crisis in 1996, the rate got cut to $11.33 an hour. This hourly rate also applied to the training employees had to take to get or keep their job, which required a minimum of 160 hours of closely monitored in-person training classes. Thus, the providers had to not only pay employees for taking the class, but they had to cover the payment to substitute staff members who took over the duties of the employees who were in class.

Unfortunately, the turnover was and remains extremely high for HTS direct care staff members. This happens because the staff members get burned out and want to transfer. Accordingly, at the agency we did everything we could to reduce turnover, since professional HTS workers are hard to get. This is the case because many work several jobs and often move away when they are offered the opportunity to receive more pay.

One of our strategies in Oklahoma to reduce turnover was to use an overtime exemption written into law within The Federal Fair Labor Standards Act. As a result, Oklahoma developmental disability providers widely used this strategy. This was certainly new and concerning to me, but as far as I could tell, everyone was satisfied with the arrangement. HTS were paid straight time, and the clients enjoyed stability. Progress for the client was truly evident with the staffing structure the exemption allowed. My skepticism about the overtime exemption was rescinded; I went to work to make sure my agency was meeting certain parameters. These included that the work is performed in a private home, where the employee did not spend more than 20 percent of their time cleaning.

Through my research, and with the help of Joni Fritz, our Wage and Hour expert at ANCOR in Washington, D.C., I became a subject matter expert on this topic. Among other things, ANCOR advocated with the U.S. Department of Labor and other federal agencies to firm up the language supporting the exemption in the Federal Fair Labor Standards Act (29 U.S.C. 213(a)(15)). At first, it looked like the Department of Labor and the federal government would make the changes, but the World Trade Center terrorist attacks that happened in September 2001 changed everything. After that, the struggle to codify the act stalled, and eventually a Federal Appeals Court ruled in 2007 that HTS does not qualify for a companionship exemption; this opinion was further solidified in 2016 by the Supreme Court.

Before all that, a Tulsa attorney sought to gain more funds for HTS employees after he found out that they were working over forty hours a week and being paid straight time.

Once the Tulsa attorney got involved, he was able to find people from many agencies across Oklahoma to file overtime lawsuits. Some of these lawsuits were fought, and some were settled. The result was an increase in expenses for the agencies serving the disabled. Not only were there increased costs for overtime pay for a single staffer, recruitment and training needed to be considered. In turn, these expenses, on top of the regular and overtime hourly wages of $11.33 and $12.80 respectively, made it exceedingly difficult for providers to maintain services to the disabled.

The parents of disabled children and teens did not always understand the difficulties we faced. For example, when ONCOR member Doug and I were lobbying in the halls of the Capitol, before the Capital Commandos were formed, we ran into two actively lobbying parents who were seeking more services for children who were developmentally disabled. Doug and I immediately introduced ourselves with our positive partnership attitude, proposing that we might join forces to be more persuasive to legislators by working together. But instead of seeing the wisdom in this approach, the parents called us "greedy providers." Further, they did not believe we were earnest in our desire to work together. Thus, they initially refused to work with us, saying, "You are only down here trying to get a rate increase, while we are here getting services for our children."

Eventually, though, we began to see the parents in committee meetings, and, after a time, we learned to respect each other, because we both realized that we all just wanted the best for everyone. Our joint lobbying efforts paid off, too; we were able to get one rate increase during the time that I was highly active with the group.

In my opinion, there was never an OKDHS Director with whom we had as great a working relationship as Director Howard Hendrick. Until the present day, that is. Currently, Secretary Justin Brown is at the helm of OKDHS. Secretary Brown is super compassionate to the needs of Oklahomans receiving services through his department and agencies. Secretary Brown and his Chief of Staff, Samantha Galloway, with the help of DDS Director Beth Scrutchins, have been championing services to Oklahomans with developmental and other disabilities by supporting providers like Rise Staffing.

With this great state-level team in place, the Oklahoma legislature provided enough money to eliminate the waiting list and increase providers' reimbursement rates. This was good news for our services.

ResCare Oklahoma was part of the Southwest Region, and we were supervised out of Austin, Texas. The Texas support was exceptional, and was a great fit for me and my management style. However, around this time the organization started to indicate that I might have to move to a different region. From my previous observations at corporate meetings and events, it was apparent the move to the new region was not going to be a good fit for me.

A fellow ONCOR member then made an offer for me to work at his company, doing legislative work and helping him expand his legislative efforts into other states. I thought about the job for a while and felt that it was an exciting opportunity.

Truth be told, at one time I thought I'd retire as a Regional Vice President for ResCare. But while setting goals and initiating action to achieve them are super important to me, being flexible and able to pivot is even more key.

I submitted my resignation to ResCare, but I continued to be the executive director of ONCOR when I moved to my new job—which led to some interesting experiences around the nation.

Working with Clients in Memphis

After I left ResCare and before I started Phoenix Residential Services, I worked briefly in Memphis at the request of my friend and employer, Doug. A government agency had recently closed an institution there, and my agency was awarded a contract to care for the institutionalized people who were affected.

While I was working in Memphis, an especially memorable experience occurred when a client had an unfortunate encounter with the police that led to his death. This experience occurred after I had been working in Memphis for a few months.

Ricky, a client that had a few behavioral issues, went out to attend a recreational event with his staff member. As they drove through the downtown area of Beale Street, Ricky became upset about something and started to attempt to run away from the staff member by opening the door of the moving car. The staff member stopped and ran after Ricky, abandoning his car, not his client. As they ran, they passed a big police station; at once, two police officers ran out, feeling they had to do something to stop Ricky. The staff member tried to stop the police by telling them that Ricky was a person with a developmental disability. As he further explained, "I work in the group home with him, so please let's work together to stop him by talking to him."

But that did not happen. Instead, one police officer grabbed the staff member, thinking he was part of some nefarious activity, and put handcuffs on him. Though the staff member tried to protest, the police officer left him on the ground. The police then left in a squad car, and eventually caught up to Ricky. When he did not immediately stop and submit, they pepper-sprayed him, handcuffed him, and threw him in the back seat of their car.

As they drove off to take him to the police station, Ricky began to vomit because of the pepper spray. Unfortunately, because his hands were tied together and he was hunched over from the way he had been shoved into the back of the car, he suffocated on his vomit. The police did not notice him struggling to breathe, so he died in the back of the police car.

I thought the police should have been responsible for his welfare once they placed him in their custody. But the police never suffered any consequences for his death. I later had to go to a lot of court hearings and investigations involving the police, the Department of Human Services, and the district attorney's office. The police officers were quickly cleared of any responsibility, and Ricky's death was attributed to his own behavior on the street and in the back of the car.

The agency's insurance company assisted us in making a settlement payment to Ricky's family. It was interesting to see the way the monetary value of Ricky's life was calculated. Basically, the negotiations centered on how much money and support Ricky would have provided to his family; that value was the basis for calculating a figure that I can't remember now—but it was a large sum of money. It made me sad to think that his family just loved him and only wanted to see some sort of responsibility taken; for them, the money was enough acknowledgment of what had occurred.

I thought that the police had culpability in Ricky's death. It seemed absurd that the settlement should come from our not-for-profit agency rather than the city, which, in my view, was more to blame and also had more money. The training of those police officers was also something we talked about in negotiations. If the officers had only taken a minute to recognize that Ricky's caretaker was not a threat, this senseless death would likely not have occurred. I must have been the only one with those thoughts, but today my thoughts are still the same.

Ohio Time

After working in Memphis, I moved on to a position in Ohio. Weird thing about time zones—my job was in Ohio, but my hotel room was in Indiana. Ohio, Eastern Time; Indiana, Central Time.

Not being a morning person, I was already one hour behind when I woke up.

But that was far from the only change I had to get used to. Ohio had quite a different service delivery system than Oklahoma and Tennessee. Ohio funded services through county boards, whereas Oklahoma and Tennessee funded through a state agency. I really enjoyed the county board approach to programs providing support. The people were friendly and the countryside was lovely, full of pretty views and beautiful old barns. The people we provided services to were ready to learn and earn. They had great support from the community as well.

As much as I liked developing policies and doing political lobbying, I never quite fit in with the new company because I had no interaction with the clients. Instead, the work involved writing up political position papers and urging state politicians to support them. By contrast, when I worked in a hospital and a center for developmentally disabled patients, I loved the one-on-one interaction with the people. I missed that at my new job. As a result, I decided to take a break from working, because I missed the direct one-on-one interaction, and I felt this time off would help me in deciding what to do next.

Meanwhile, during this break from work in the field, I had a lawn care business and a screen-printing company called Indigo Images, so I worked on building these companies. I loved screen printing since it was a physical job. The job also helped me understand that I had to be patient, and it gave me a lot of time to think about what I wanted to do next. At the same time, mowing lawns and screen printing at Indigo Images helped me earn the money I needed to do what I decided to do next—open my own agency in Oklahoma to help the developmentally disabled find and train for jobs.

Once I decided to open my agency, I had to get a contract with the state of Oklahoma's Developmental Disabilities Division. To do so, I had to fill out a lot of paperwork and show that I had some money in the bank. The state required this information to demonstrate that I was a reputable company and had sufficient financing in place to cover the costs of launching the agency.

I had to submit my application to the state of Oklahoma to get a contract to become a provider five times. Each time I had to provide additional information and supporting documents. I finally provided everything the state wanted and was able to launch my company—Phoenix Residential Services. I named it after the phoenix bird, an immortal bird in Greek mythology and the mythology of many other cultures. As an immortal creature, it repeatedly regenerates itself and is born again. It is also associated with the sun and obtains new life by arising from the ashes of its predecessor. It is a symbol of change, growth, and renewal.

That is what I hoped to be able to offer; this bird symbolized what I knew my clients could do when they wanted to change their lives. The phoenix also represented the changes that needed to be made in the way these clients were perceived in society. Many stories written about them are inaccurate or simply not true, focusing on ways their handicaps prevent them from doing things rather than focusing on the many things they can, or can learn to do.

I rented a small office on Broadway in Sand Springs, Oklahoma, saying to myself, "If you build it, they will come," just as Kevin Costner did in *Field of Dreams.*

The plan was to build the agency to provide services to clients who received in-home support through waivers from the state of Oklahoma. The in-home support waiver (IHSW) helps pay for people to be cared for in their homes in the community.

Although the IHSW has a lower reimbursement rate from the state than other waivered services, I figured that if I got a lot of the people getting these waivers, the volume would make up for this low rate. Also, I knew that the larger providers did not have time for these small cases, so I would be able to offer much-needed services to my new clients. It would be a win for everybody involved.

CHAPTER 4

Building A Waivered Services Agency: Introducing Phoenix

Though I was still working in the same field that I had for many years at that point, starting an agency was a brand new experience for me. There were so many new decisions to make, and new responsibilities on my shoulders. But it was a thrilling and rewarding experience from the very beginning.

Creating Phoenix Residential Services

The agency was called Phoenix Residential Services because we focused on helping the developmentally disabled find housing and become integrated into the community. This focus helped to provide them with the foundation they needed to find a job.

I originally started thinking about creating the agency back when I was part of ANCOR's board of directors. Several of my peers had opened agencies because, much like me, they had a heart for the business, or because they had a child with a disability. As I did, they took their home equity and put the money from it into the bank to start their agency. While some people established non-profits, several of them warned me that a non-profit must have a board of directors. At first, this board could be composed of friends and people in the community who I knew would support the growth of the agency. However, I was advised that as these people retired, new people would replace them on the board; these people may not have the same priorities for the agency, and may not know or appreciate that I had started the agency with my own money. This could potentially become difficult to manage.

I decided to set up Phoenix Residential Services as a for-profit agency. The only difference from a non-profit is that I would not be able to have tax deductions or get donations. While this might seem to put my company at a disadvantage, the big advantage was that I would be able to retain complete ownership of the company.

Becoming the full owner meant that I took on even more responsibility than I had at ResCare, or when I worked in Memphis and Ohio. Among other things, as a company owner, I was responsible if people did not show up or if they did a bad job. So, I had to be incredibly careful about who I was going to hire to work with me. Fortunately, I was lucky with most of the staff people I hired when first creating my team.

Working with Some Clients at Phoenix

One of my key employees was Janie Risley, a former kindergarten and first grade special education teacher at a local elementary school. Several of her old clients looked her up and became customers of Phoenix Residential Services. One of her major contributions was creating an arts and crafts program, and she led one of its biggest activities—a Craft Day, where different clients joined us in creating arts and crafts objects. It was a blast for everyone who participated.

The agency's clients were very appreciative of our help, too. One of them was Laurie Winiecke, a client with autism who is still a good friend to this day. She was about eleven when I first met her. We were still small, and, as the owner of the agency, I got to be Laurie's HTS. Laurie's dad worked near my office, so he dropped her off in the morning; I then led her in a day full of activities, from swimming at public pools to fishing in the river to going to different summer day camps.

We furnished the office with comfortable couches, chairs, and photos on the walls, so it was warm and welcoming for both the clients and their parents.

Readers, we cannot talk about Phoenix Residential Services and leave out Amos. Amos and I became acquainted while working at ResCare. Amos used to live at the Hissom Memorial Center. He married a local woman who had two children, and he became their stepfather. I originally got to know this family because they had several pets, and they were having a tough time finding a new place to rent. Property owners balked because of the children and the pets. The best course of action for Amos and his family was to cooperate with their current property owner, a lovely human named Robert Moglenecki. Amos and his family cooperated, and through this episode we all became friends.

Amos and his family were interested in buying their own home. To do so, Amos and his wife had to save and curb spending; it was excruciating to help them get through it. Amos had a big team of people supporting him, but only he and his wife controlled the money in and out of their household. Amos did receive a monthly room and board payment from his settlement with the Hissom lawsuit. That steady income, along with saving, budgeting, and consistent earning, allowed them to buy their own home. Caroline Thompson and Neely Shaw of Midtown Mortgage were super helpful to Amos and his team throughout the process. Neely and Caroline also helped two other Phoenix Residential clients purchase their own homes.

For a time, Amos drove his own car and lifeguarded at the YMCA in Tulsa. Later, after his eyesight began failing and he was listed as legally blind, he could no longer drive or serve as a lifeguard—but he could still do things, like woodworking and other repair jobs. I helped him find many jobs over the fifteen years we worked together.

Amos was also a big part of the holiday season. Thanksgiving is my favorite holiday. I really like it. I love the Macy's Thanksgiving Day Parade, which features a float at the end with Santa Claus. To me, that indicates that it's time to start celebrating Christmas and the holiday season. I also like this holiday because it always falls around my birthday. At some point, the staff and I got the idea for a gala celebration to observe all the festivity. Amos and his wife dressed up as Santa and Ms. Claus every year for this dinner.

The event proved a big hit with the clients of the agency, too; we had full attendance at our first event and at every single one thereafter. The first one, held at the Sand Springs Community Center, was especially hilarious because I bought pre-made turkey dinners from a local grocery store without realizing that the turkeys were frozen. So, I had to use several ovens—my own, my neighbor's, and one staff member's—to get the turkeys cooked in time for a dinner with about forty people.

Despite this initial hiccup, the Thanksgiving Dinner grew from year to year. At each dinner, we had door prizes and gifts for the staff, who came wearing logos for the agency, which featured the phoenix bird.

I also created a longevity awards program as an incentive for staff members. The staff members who worked for me for three years got a ring and necklace with the phoenix on it. At five years, staff members received a ring and necklace with a gemstone on it. Some staff members liked these items so much that they still wear these rings and necklaces today.

Phoenix Residential Services started with the in-home support waiver program, which required a consistent provider who could work with cases that received ten to twenty hours of service a week. One of my most inspiring experiences was meeting a client named

Lisa. Lisa delighted me every week when she reported on how much she learned to do for herself. This was inspiring because some of the parents of our clients had not taken the initiative to train their child in even the most basic activities of daily living, including doing laundry, paying for groceries at the store, or cleaning the house. The staff members and I had to teach them these things so that they could live on their own in an apartment or house. Lisa was such an inspiration because she often called us up to describe her latest accomplishments. For example, she would call and say, "This is Lisa, and guess what I did? I just paid for my own groceries and got the change back."

It was similarly inspiring to hear other clients describe their accomplishments. One client let me know that he did his laundry and folded the sheets by himself. Still others described many things they learned to do for themselves, which enabled them to live independently.

I found learning about these milestones exciting, because it showed how our work teaching and training our clients contributed to their growth and made a substantial difference in their lives. Seeing this progress and the improvements in our clients' lives is why I loved this program.

Because of our small staff size we were limited in the number of people we could serve, even though most people worked forty to sixty hours a week. Everyone put in a lot of effort to handle the workload, as the houses with clients with supportive living arrangements required staff members to be available to help 24/7. We were required to provide 4.2 staff people per household on a single shift, or up to seven people for a long shift. This staffing problem affects the entire industry that provides supportive living assistance across the country.

Our company kept growing as we picked up a lot of supported living cases and hired more and more staff to handle these new clients. As a result, after I had over 120 employees, I had to move out of my little first office and into the entire second floor of the State Farm building in Sand Springs.

Footprints in My Heart

I had some wonderful experiences with the parents and clients that I worked with. One of these experiences was with a father-daughter combo I fell in love with after I met them while networking at an event in Bartlesville. Robert came over to me with his daughter Nora; as they walked over, I could see that she was disabled from the way she dragged her feet and dangled her arms. Robert explained that Nora had cerebral palsy and was the daughter of his first wife, although they were long divorced; he had since married a woman from the Philippines who had a five-year-old son from a previous relationship. Now, as he explained, Nora was in her sophomore year of high school and needed help. "I need someone to be at home for her, since I have to go to work," he told me.

I soon found a good match for Nora's needs in one of my staff members, Kathy, who lived only a couple of blocks away from them. Both Nora and her dad loved her. Since Kathy lived so close, she was able to walk through the ice and snow to take care of Nora. She even braved the elements one year when there was a freezing ice storm, and she dodged falling trees and walked on five-inch-thick ice to get to Nora's house. She did so because she wanted to make sure Nora was comfortable, could use the restroom and shower, and had all her personal care needs taken care of. Also, Kathy did these things for Nora because she knew it was hard for Nora's father to handle these tasks, as he was a war veteran who had a very bad back.

Eventually, Kathy did such an excellent job caring for Nora that my agency nominated her for the Direct Support Professional of the Year award with the Developmental Disabilities Division. When she won, Nora, Robert, and Kathy went to Oklahoma City to receive the award. They felt it was an incredibly special moment when Nora's name was called, and she went to the front of the room to receive the award. Nora beamed as she received it, and everyone in the audience clapped heartily.

When Nora began going to high school, she needed to have physical help during the school day to use the restroom and do her personal care. Nora found that it was extremely uncomfortable using the restroom at school because the school staffers used a tool called a "wand" to clean Nora's private areas. The wand reminded me of a Swiffer duster, but with toilet paper instead of Swiffer pads. So let me say this plainly, a plastic stick with toilet paper tucked into its end gets wedged between Nora's legs to refresh her after relieving herself. Nora was not comfortable, and even reported being injured by this assistance. She was also not comfortable with the person doing the "wanding," and suspected that the lady did not like doing this job. Nora said the aide did not want to wait long enough to allow Nora to do it herself, as she did at home.

Thus, she asked Robert and me to come to a meeting with the principal and school superintendent, with the hope that she could get different assistance in the restroom. But as much as her father and I tried to persuade the superintendent and the principal to change their policies, they refused. Nora, her father, and I left the meeting feeling very frustrated that she was not allowed to have a voice or gain any more independence, though she vowed to manage this setback.

About three weeks later, tragedy struck. Nora was walking on the school track, getting ready for a Special Olympics event that she had been excitedly looking forward to participating in. But her father called me in tears, and choked out the words, "Nora dropped dead walking on the track at school."

I was speechless for a moment, before I was able to tell Robert how sad I was for him. As I hung up, I thought about how he and Nora had such a strong love for each other, which I'd observed over the four years I worked with them. Nora had a happy family and home life, and she and her father had a strong father-daughter relationship. It was heartbreaking to learn that she had suddenly died so young.

But why did her sudden death happen? I later found out that Nora had been taking a birth control pill called YAZ, which led to a blood clot that caused her heart to stop. Her death was sudden, and it was very traumatic for her fellow students who were nearby when it happened, as well as for all the people that knew and worked with her. Later, I learned that the drug, manufactured by Bayer AG, was subject to many lawsuits alleging the YAZ pills not only caused blood clots, but also gallbladder problems, heart attacks, and strokes.

Chaining

Over the years, my job has been chock full of training techniques. The one that is most imprinted on my way of training is called "chaining." There is straight chaining, backward chaining, and total chaining. Hold on—am I talking about actual chains and holding somebody down? No, I am not. I am talking about a training technique that involves deeply analyzing a task, breaking it down into steps, and then teaching those steps to a person in one of the three ways mentioned above.

One of my favorite task analysis and chaining exercises is how to make a peanut butter and jelly sandwich. With not that much time—say, ten or fifteen minutes max—you have to plan out how to teach a person who has never made a peanut butter and jelly sandwich how to make one.

To do this, you must start with what you may not consider serious tasks—like taking the tie off the bread bag, and then taking the bread out of the bag. It can be surprising, and sometimes even hilarious, if you do not provide the most minute details—for example, grabbing the bread bag *gently*, because someone may very well squeeze the entire loaf of bread, making the task irrelevant. So before using this method with a client, you really must break it down, practice the tasks in your analysis, and get a coworker to test it to make sure you have all the steps.

Let me give you some more information on chaining.

Backward Chaining: Backward chaining involves teaching a behavioral chain beginning with the last step. This means that you would demonstrate the entire chain of behaviors except for the last step, which you would then allow the client to perform. Using the PB&J example, the trainer completes every single step, except for the last one—say, cutting the sandwich in half—which the trainee would do, and then get the sandwich as a reward! Backward chaining will work if the trainee may have an easier time learning the steps at the end of the behavior chain first, rather than those at the beginning. It also has the advantage of creating a strong link between the work and the reinforcement. So, most of the work (observed by the trainee) leads to the biggest reinforcement (consuming the food). Once the last step is mastered at an independent level, you can move to teaching the last two steps, then the last three steps, etc.

Forward chaining: Forward chaining involves teaching a behavioral chain beginning with the first step; you have the trainee complete the first step independently, and then demonstrate all remaining steps. Forward chaining is recommended if the trainee displays momentum to complete more steps at the start of the behavior chain. Forward chaining has the advantage of using behavior momentum, since the first step in a process is often the simplest, easiest step. In the PB&J example, the trainee might get the bread out of the breadbox independently, and then you would prompt every other step. Once the first step is mastered at an independent level, you move to the first two steps, then the first three steps, etc.

Total task chaining: Total task chaining is when you teach a complete behavior chain, one step after another. This is the method that most teachers or parents naturally use to teach a skill. For example: "Okay, turn the water on ... Now soap up your hands ... Good, now scrub your hands together..." The adult walks the child through each step, prompting as necessary. But for some people, this may be too complex of a teaching style. For that reason, backward or forward chaining is usually more commonly used.

Task analysis and chaining was a lifesaver when I started job coaching. Task analysis sounds complicated and detail-oriented—two things I normally try to avoid, because of the way my brain works. But it turns out that task analysis isn't as complicated as it might sound. It's simply explaining the step-by-step directions to completing a skill. A task analysis is typically created by completing the skill yourself, or by watching someone else do it. It's important to not just write up a task analysis based on your memory. Even simple tasks, like making a PB&J sandwich, can have small but important steps that you may inadvertently skip.

Once I got started, I realized that having the steps written out and knowing exactly what to do is a good thing. It made me feel more comfortable teaching, because I knew what I was doing thanks to my task analysis. If I, as a job coach, do not teach a step, then I really cannot blame the trainee for not completing that step. Thank goodness for the internet, and for the opportunity to consult with professionals to gain more detail on how to perform specific tasks.

Professionals in the field of autism began teaching us about applied behavioral analysis (ABA) to promote learning and meaningful change based on an individual's specific needs. There is a lot more to ABA, but chaining is a big part of every lesson. Thinking back on it, chaining has been a foundational tool in my current job coaching techniques.

I'd like to give a few more examples of this technique. Once I had a lady who wanted to work at McDonald's; however, she could not for the life of her stop hugging people or touching them. You could advise her not to hug people and explain that it's not professional, and then within ten minutes she'd be hugging people again. In order to help her get the job she wanted, we had to figure something out.

We noticed that while she was very good at the beginning of any task, her commitment eventually wore down. But the one thing she always stuck to was music and dancing, particularly Jazzercise. So we found a class offered by the senior services; they were willing to let her come over and do some volunteering like dusting and cleaning, and in exchange she got to attend the Jazzercise class. After she began the class and liked it, we went a step further. Her volunteer duties expanded to handing out cards to the people as they entered the class; the cards said things like "Do Jazzercise so you can eat more doughnuts." But we also instructed her to not hug people as she handed out the cards.

Because the Jazzercise class was a strong incentive, she worked hard to stop hugging people—and in this way, she got more accustomed to interacting with people without hugging or touching them. Eventually she stopped the hugging and went on to get the job she wanted. So that was a great example of how backward chaining can help prepare someone to be independent. We started with an exciting reinforcement at the beginning—Jazzercise—and in this case, backward chaining meant zooming forward toward her goals.

I had another person who had so many behaviors that he was double-staffed—meaning he had two people with him almost twenty-four hours a day. His impairments made him dangerous to himself, others, and his surroundings. In time I learned that many of this man's behaviors were a result of the fact that some of the people working with him did not understand his self-image. He felt that he was the head of the household, and he wanted things to be done in a certain way and to understand what was happening around him, as any adult would. But he was not treated that way; he was treated like a child, never knowing what his schedule was, who would be in his house, or where he was going when he was taken out.

We came up with a system that helped him to understand and anticipate what was happening around him, in his limited but nonetheless perceptive way. This was very exciting to him, and his dangerous behaviors basically stopped—all because communication started.

Guess what, readers? I got fired from that case. Why? Because we were successful in communicating with this person, and nobody wanted that to happen. It still breaks my heart, because that's exactly what we're there for. So many of the clients we work with are frustrated at the things that obstruct their ability to communicate, and it can be such a joy to figure out how to remove some of those obstacles and talk to that person and help them feel empowered about their life. That's when the amazing changes happen.

Being unable to know what is happening in your life from minute to minute is horrendous. Imagine waking up to a stranger in your house. That's right—on any given day a brand new staff person you've never met before could be standing in your bedroom, bossing you around. Ideally, each person receiving services should meet, interview, and approve of the staff that works for them. But because staff can be hard to find, new people sometimes just show up. At my agency, we do not practice this method of staffing. We go above and beyond to make sure everyone knows who will be working with them, what they'll be doing, and where it will happen. Helping that man gain some control in his life by simply allowing him to know what was going to happen to him is one of my favorite success stories.

CHAPTER 5
Training Staff To Create Fulfilling Job Matches

Even though Phoenix Residential Services was focused on preparing people with disabilities to find jobs was always at the top of my mind. I knew I wanted my agency to shift its mission to primarily supporting people via job training and placement. But to do so, it would be critical to find the right staffing and train them properly. I had to find people who were empathetic to individuals with disabilities and committed to working closely with them; this would be key to equipping job seekers with the necessary training and support to feel confident that they could do a job—and convince a potential employer that they could do it, too. Accordingly, I had to make my expectations clear to my staff.

What I Tell Prospective and New Staff Members about What to Expect

Warning: this section contains explicit information. Not pleasant, but factual nonetheless.

Staffing has always been an issue because of the difficulties staffers regularly face in working with the disabled. They must know what to expect and feel fully confident they have the skills and the emotional make-up to handle the job. Most people do not want to take care of another person's most intimate bodily needs. Additionally, people with developmental and other disabilities commonly have behavioral issues, resulting in physical attacks on staff members. For example, they may punch, scratch, pull hair, spit, and even use their feces and urine as weapons. A prospective staff member needs to be able to deal with such behavior if they want to jump into this field.

Staff members also need to be prepared for such behaviors suddenly occurring, even after their relationship with a given client seems to be going smoothly. It's possible that even after spending a lot of time with a client, getting to know and like them, and feeling successful about the work, problem behavior can still happen.

Whenever a physical attack happens, a staff member must deal with whatever horrible thing occurred and continue to work with that client after the attack is over. There will always be procedures in place to support them, but it's important that even in that stressful time they remember their responsibility to the client.

When I interview people for this job, I take care to ensure that there is a good fit between their reason for wanting the job and their understanding of the requirements. For example, over the years, many staff members who have gone on to be successful on the job have told me that they like to do the work because they are a people person and enjoy working with people. While that is a good sign, they have to understand that this work goes beyond just meeting and talking comfortably with people. That's because the job requires them to be willing to fully dedicate themselves to helping others, with no expectation of any form of appreciation from those they help.

As I explain, sometimes staff members may start to feel tired of doing all the things they do to help a client and getting no thanks in return, even though they feel they have been truly giving of themselves in providing compassionate care. I tell prospective staffers, "You are not going to feel appreciated when such an incident occurs."

Additionally, in assessing whether someone is a good fit for the job, when someone tells me they like to work with people, I ask them to examine whether they feel they have a hole in their life that they're trying to fill by doing this feel-good work. If that is the case, I ask them to take a hard look at themselves before going to work in this field. I want them to carefully assess their motives. I've seen people who have had something broken in their life and think that they can fill that void by working with a disabled client; then, when it doesn't work out and they fail at the job, because they were not truly up to it, they can wind up feeling resentment toward the client, other staffers, and themselves.

Then, when such a person leaves the job, their client has no staff member until I can find a replacement, which can take several days or weeks. Thus, if people come to this field with a hole they need to fill, I tell them that this is not the place to fill that void; we need people who are already whole to work with the clients who need their help.

We also must be concerned about the background of anyone working with our clients. We conduct a thorough background check, including national fingerprint checks, to ensure no one who has a shady or violent past gets in to work with us.

The Experience and Training Needed to Work with the Developmentally Disabled

When hiring and working with new staff members, I also look for people who have had certain types of experience before I provide additional training for the job.

Most importantly, to do this work, people need to have experience dealing with disabled individuals and the problems they face. They can't have a queasy stomach, because they will have to deal with bodily functions such as feces, urine, vomit, blood, and mucus, much like a nurse or doctor would, even though this is not a medical profession. For example, they might have to deal with these bodily functions if the client has a medical crisis due to an illness or injury.

If an illness or injury does occur, the staff member may have to take their client to a doctor or to the hospital; in either case, the staffer must stay with the client during their medical treatment.

In general, what I think makes a competent staff member, and what I look for in deciding whether to hire someone, is not only having the right skills and a positive, caring attitude, but also having a well-rounded life experience. In other words, a good staffer is someone who does well in managing their own life and has good people skills. For instance, this might be someone who has successfully raised children or is skilled at training pets, which shows their propensity for helping others. They should also have helped others consistently throughout their life, so they have had some life experiences that are compatible with working in this field. Teachers come in all shapes and sizes, and we never know who they will be and when they will cross our paths. Over the years I have recruited employees in many different situations. Once on a plane back to Tulsa I met a person who wound up coming to work direct care part-time. This person worked with me for a long time and is still a friend.

CHAPTER 6
Thinking About A Change

Phoenix Residential Services was at its peak. Our office took up a full floor of our building, and we had a large staff and lots of business. We were caring for over 120 customers. During this time I also opened a home health agency called Ellen Bee Home Care.

You can imagine running a business that operated twenty-four hours a day along with a separate home care agency is a lot of work. Yes, I was becoming exhausted. I was tired, and I was doing a lot of it by myself. Yes, I had staff, even management I trusted, but I was the ultimate person in charge. I was getting burnt out and not enjoying the job.

Something had to change. I started talking about innovative ideas and a new direction for the agency. Just at that time, the RN heading up Ellen Bee gave her notice. When that happened, I decided to divest myself from the home care business.

My friendly competitor Bios Corporation also had a home care division. I respected them, so I called them up and said that I was thinking of closing Ellen Bee. Did they want my customers? Yes, they were happy to help, and I so appreciate the care they took to help transition the patients from Ellen Bee to A Better Life Home Care.

Next, I had a hair-pulling and emotional meeting with my accountant, Amanda. Amanda pointed out where we were struggling with our budget. The twenty-four-hour-a-day homes were draining any chance of profit, especially because of overtime costs. We worked on the numbers, and the inevitable solution became clear—release the twenty-four-hour-a-day homes to focus attention on the service that inspired me. Vocational services are the inspiration for change.

Now armed with a plan and a secure feeling of purpose, I was able to start asking my twenty-four-hour homes to find another agency. During that period we were also busy looking for vocational opportunities that we could develop, so we started an initiative called the PODS—People Out Doing Service.

The Beginning of Rise Staffing

True to its name, the Phoenix transformed itself and Rise Staffing was born. Wow—this was exciting, and it gave me new motivation for my work. Most people were gracious about the fact that we were not going to continue providing twenty-four-hour residential support services. Some were not so gracious, mostly I think because they did not want to make a change. Finding a new agency is difficult, and my staff and I helped these folks transition as much as possible.

We developed a new logo that set the style for the agency. Rise Staffing's new office was in the Centenary United Methodist Church in downtown Tulsa, a beautiful 1920s structure with wonderful Art Deco lines; we decided to follow the theme and design our office to complement the church's architecture. My sister-in-law, Victoria McGoffin, offered to help me with the design. She absolutely nailed it—our office was gorgeous. Lots of sweat, blood, and tears went into the execution of the remodel. We kept the old office running in Sand Springs while we renovated our space in the church to accommodate our new operation.

When we started, the floors were covered with a crazy shag and the walls were purple. When we finished, the floor was concrete with black and gold embellishments, the walls royal blue and white with black trim. Victoria painted us an eight-foot-by-four-foot Art Deco painting of Tulsa's Philtower Building. She also refined my logo and painted it on a large board. Tulsa Tech-Sand Springs Campus' Digital Art program digitized the logo and created several vinyl pieces for the walls. The students did the work for free, and, somehow, we were gifted the materials by Julie Spears of Tulsa Tech. We will never forget Julie and her students' kindness and support.

We had a big open house to show off our hard work, but our biggest pride was in the People Out Doing Services program. We were able to highlight the program to state case managers, other providers, client families and friends, customers, and community members. Everyone showed up to support us. We were also excited because the state of Oklahoma had donated a lift to the program, and the church gave us a special room that we could use as what we called a changing place. It was decorated in a cowboy chic sort of way that made it pleasant for just about anyone to come in, change, take a break from their wheelchair, or do whatever they needed. We had a changing table, a bunch of changing supplies, gloves, the lift, music, lights, and sensory items, because it was not only a changing place but also a sensory space for the people we worked with who had autism.

CHAPTER 7

How The Rise Staffing Vocational Services Agency Works

Since Rise Staffing, originally called Phoenix Residential Services, has been successful since 2004—twenty years now!—I want to describe a little about how the agency works. On the one hand, it is a vocational service that puts people to work, resulting in paychecks for the staff members and clients who find jobs; at the same time, as an administrator, I had to figure out a way that our company could make a profit at the same rate that others in the recruitment industry do. Traditionally, people have been slow to establish vocational services, due to a low revenue return.

Rise Staffing has been something of an exception to that rule, because we discovered a way to have job coaches work with more than one client at the same time in a one-to-one situation. We produced what we call PODS, which stands for People out Doing Service, in which a single staff member can work with five or six clients at a time. Aside from being profitable, we have been able to place a lot more people in jobs this way.

Using this approach, we built up a successful vocational service model with a profit of up to $635.58 per week per client, which reflects the profit the company makes after deducting an administrative fee. This amount is much greater than the average earnings of Oklahoma providers, who average $17.76 per hour for providing one-to-one services and $4.50 per hour for running training work-shops for developmentally disabled individuals.

The Importance of Providing Vocational Services

In providing these services, Rise Staffing has filled a critical need for helping a large developmentally disabled population. For example, there are over ten thousand disabled individuals in Oklahoma alone. To help this population, the Developmental Disabilities Service Division (DDS) offers home and community-based waivers to help people receive services. While about three thousand of them are listed as receiving services, 5,409 Oklahomans are on the DDS waiver waitlist.

As Rise Staffing grows, it can provide help for more clients. It has been an established contract provider for DDS for more than fifteen years. It was first a contract provider as Phoenix Residential Services; after its name change and shift to focus on employment services, it has been listed as Tulsa's newest niche employment agency. At that time, we obtained a vocational contract with the Oklahoma Department of Rehabilitation Services.

Working with Partners and Volunteers

Another way that Rise Staffing provides extra value to clients is that it partners with existing community organizations and draws on the services of volunteers.

- **Partnering with Existing Community Organizations.** The advantage of partnering with community organizations is that the relationship can be mutually beneficial. For example, a community organization already has a loyal membership interested in the activities and services it organizes. As a result, the members of a community group can prove to be very receptive to whatever the group offers to or seeks from members, such as volunteering to help the company better provide its services. In this case, Rise has partnered with the Centenary United Methodist Church. It's possible for companies to form partnerships with multiple organizations; however, for a small company like Rise Staffing, it's ideal to keep the number of partners to no more than three.

- **Using Volunteers to Help with Providing Services.** Volunteers can be a wonderful way to cut down costs and provide services to far more clients than would otherwise be possible. With some training and shadowing of a regular staffer, a volunteer can soon do the work. The process is a little like starting as a medical intern working in a hospital ward. In Rise Staffing's case, we have worked with numerous community volunteer organizations. Our mission in doing so is to maximize the number of clients we assist with coaching, counseling, and day-to-day job training. With more volunteers, we can provide more services to more individuals, although we do need to take care to train the volunteers well so they know clearly what to do and how to do it.

Training Job Coaches and Employment Specialists

For staff members to consistently provide services to clients, I developed a process called Customized Job Developmental to ensure that clients are appropriately matched to an employer and position.

This process, which consists of four steps, is summarized in the chart on the following page.

CUSTOMIZED JOB DEVELOPMENT

PROCESS OF MATCHING STRENGTHS, NEEDS, INTERESTS, AND SKILLS OF A JOB SEEKER WITH NEEDS OF AN EMPLOYER

STEP 1: DISCOVERY - JOB SEEKER CENTERED

- Conduct interviews
- Go on home visits
- Job shadow
- Take business tours
- Make observations in various environments
- Create vocational profile with job development team members

STEP 2: JOB PLANNING

- Identify vocational interests
- List employers based upon interests
- Work environment observations
- Meet with employers
- Discuss opportunities to match job seeker profile with employer needs

STEP 3: JOB DEVELOPMENT

- Job Negotiation - discuss tasks, pay, supports, hours
- Schedule tours, informational and working interviews
- Observations by job coach
- Job shadow
- Training and support

STEP 4: PLACEMENT - SUPPORT AND FEEDBACK

- First 5 days - Full support
- Weekly check-ins with Job Coach
- At 4 weeks - Begin fade out
- Follow-up at 8 weeks, 12 weeks, 3 months
- Depending on contract, job seeker may graduate at 3 months

Rise Staffing | www.risestaffing.net

Placement, Support, and Feedback

After a successful placement, a staffer's job does not end. Now, they are responsible for providing the client with support and feedback for the first five days. As the client is first encountering the tasks and responsibilities that are part of their job, the staffer will be there in case they need some help in understanding what to do. The client may also need some encouragement to know that they are up to the job. Thus, the staffer must provide full support during this critical five-day period, which includes offering feedback on what the client has done well and where they need to improve.

After this five-day intensive period, the staffer should set up weekly check-ins with the job coach. This is a chance to ask the client how things are going and what he or she has been doing. Importantly, the client should be asked about any areas where they need help. If there are any personality clashes or problems that have emerged, the client should feel free to openly share them so that the staffer or job coach can provide insights on what to do to overcome the issue.

This check-in period should continue for about four weeks. After that, the staffer can begin to fade out, based on the client's ability to do the job. As necessary, the staffer can deal with any issues that come up by talking to other employees or supervisors.

At this stage, the staffer should have follow-up check-ins at eight weeks, twelve weeks, and three months. In some cases, depending on the work contract, the job seeker may graduate at the three-month mark, or they may be asked to continue the job. There even may be possibilities for a promotion if the client is doing an excellent job.

These are the steps that staffers are trained to follow for a successful placement; today, many staffers have gone through the program and are now working at Rise Staffing.

It may seem that there are a lot of steps to learn how to effectively make a job placement, and that a lot of time is needed to help each individual through the process. However, this kind of training and practice is necessary for staffers to become successful recruiters and help place developmentally disabled individuals into jobs that they will enjoy and thrive in. Accordingly, I strongly advise new staff members that to achieve the best outcome they must work through the process many times. I tell them, "Do not skimp on using the tools I am providing. You will be a better job developer and coach if you follow this advice."

Developing the Approach to Matching Clients to Jobs

The job-matching approach that I use for my clients is based on the way I personally look for a job. Knowing the things that are exciting to me and finding a good fit between my interests and abilities has always helped me find jobs that I like. This method can be a clever way to help other people find jobs that are good fits for them.

As critical as it is for a job developer to zero in on what people are happiest doing, it is important to consider their abilities too, since job seekers can be interested in a lot of things, and they may often be good at doing the things that interest them—but not always. Thus, it is important to do both—find what people are interested in *and* what they are good at doing (or what they like and can be readily trained to do).

The principle of making a match between interest and ability had become like a mantra for Rise Staffing job developers, because this is the key to making successful job placements—matching people with jobs that can make them happy. This became a passion for those I have hired to work at Rise Staffing.

Job Development Strategies

Our approach involves using the following job development strategies:

- Develop a list of twenty employers based on the three vocational areas of interest that have been identified for the job seeker.
- Use informational interviews to meet with employers to learn about the work that might be a fit for the job seeker's interests and abilities, and will also fill a need for the employer.
- Establish that the job seeker agrees with all parts of any job developmental planning; in other words, determine that the job seeker wants a job based on his or her key interests and abilities.
- Spend time with the personal support team—friends, relatives, family, or neighbors—who have contacts and have developed strong relationships with others in the community (sometimes called having social capital); even though it takes extra time to do this groundwork, the effort is worth it.
- Be a detective in actively asking questions and following leads to find job opportunities for job seekers.

The Septic Tank Caper

I had no idea what I was getting myself into when I decided to take on the seemingly simple job of repairing my septic lateral lines. But what I thought would be a day-long project soon turned into a three-week endeavor.

At first, I tried to do the job myself but quickly realized that it was more complicated than I thought, and that I didn't have the right tools or knowledge to get the job done.

So, I enlisted the help of a handyman who had different abilities than me. He was knowledgeable and experienced in many areas of home repair, though not including septic lateral lines. We then called in a professional who was able to identify and repair the problem areas in my lateral lines quickly and successfully—much faster than it would have taken me without them.

It turned out that Mr. Smith, our expert, needed a helper for his business. You guessed it, readers—the friend I'd asked to help me landed the job. Now he knows a lot about septic tank systems. They built tanks from concrete at the shop in Kellyville, Oklahoma. Eventually, my friend started operating the backhoe, and Mr. Smith had it a little easier with his help. In fact, he and Mr. Smith worked together for seventeen years, until Mr. Smith sold the business and my friend retired.

The experience taught me a lot about septic systems and lateral line maintenance along the way—things that will come in handy if I ever need similar repairs again in the future.

But the biggest takeaway is to never stop developing jobs. This was the most unique accidental job development I've ever been involved with. Nothing would have happened, nothing would have changed that day, if I didn't advocate for a job at that time. This technique does not always work out, but that has never stopped me from asking. The answer is always no if you don't ask the question.

Seventeen years of work, friendship, and business success, all from a question: Need any helpers, Mr. Smith? Frank is available!

CHAPTER 8
Job Search And Helping Clients Prepare For New Jobs

Over the years, I and my staff at Rise Staffing have developed a number of systems for conducting job searches and helping our clients prepare to begin their new jobs. These systems have allowed us to help many people with disabilities since the company launched two decades ago.

Tools for Doing a Job Search

Once job developers know their client's needs, they are ready to begin the job search process to find suitable jobs for them. To this end, they are trained to practice the following steps:

First, look for jobs already posted. Read the job description and research the target employer. Learn who's who, and what the company stands for. It is possible to do this online, by interviewing known customers of the company, and by visiting the business in person.

A first visit can be undercover, with the job developer visiting the business as a customer. This can be an effective way to observe and evaluate the environment and assess whether it is a good fit for the job seeker.

Do an informational interview to determine the atmosphere of the working environment and to find out what the coworkers are like. The purpose of this interview is not to ask for a job; instead, you should focus on evaluating the job conditions so that you can subsequently make a good match for the job seeker if a job becomes available at the company.

Consider whether a new role might be developed to help the company beyond whatever jobs may currently be available. For example, if it seems like the company could use more customers, an employee might be hired to help with outreach. If the facilities of the company look like they could use some repairs or cleaning, you might suggest that the job seeker could do this.

Practice doing these informational interviews and evaluations before going out to conduct a real interview in the field. Two job developers can practice together, using a buddy system to practice and improve.

Be a guerrilla job developer. This means that whenever and wherever you go to search for potential job openings, think about how well a particular job or company might fit a current or future client. For example, ask yourself: "Does this place look like somewhere that my client could work?" or "Would this be a good place for a job placement if I later get a client who can do this kind of work?"

Some Considerations Affecting an Individual's Ability to Obtain or Maintain Employment

After establishing the client's interests and abilities and motivating the client to *want* a job, a staff member needs to consider certain factors that may affect the ability of an individual to get a particular job and to perform it successfully. These concerns can be particularly salient in the case of a worker who is developmentally disabled, since he or she may encounter some resistance or hostility from other workers, even if the main employer is supportive.

Developing an understanding of the job environment can affect whether it is appropriate to place a client with certain disabilities into a particular job, or whether more follow-up is needed to make sure that person can effectively fit into the workplace environment.

Major considerations include the following:

- **The Environment.** The concern here is whether a given workplace will offer a welcoming and supportive environment, where coworkers are helpful and friendly. They'll need to be receptive to working with someone with a disability. While a supportive employer can help pave the way for success, it is up to the co-workers to be receptive and help the client thrive on a daily basis. If it seems that this may be a hurdle, it may be better to look for another job placement. This is an important consideration, since problems with other employees can lead to a setback—the client may not only wind up leaving the job, they may also feel a loss of self-confidence and resist other employment opportunities in the future.

- **Communication Issues.** It is necessary to consider the client's ability to communicate with others, which can affect both job performance and acceptance by their colleagues. Accordingly, it is important to take into consideration the client's skill level in speaking to others. Then, too, it is necessary to consider how willing the employer and co-workers will be to communicate with a client who may have some difficulties in speaking. They may need to listen more carefully to a client's slow speech, be patient with speech errors, and be willing to put in effort to communicate and work with a client with such disabilities.

106

- **Additional Communication Problems.** Communication problems may occur not only on account of the client's speech abilities, but also because of the nature of some clients' communication. For example, some clients may have a very literal use of language, so they may not understand when employers or co-workers make casual conversation or tell jokes. Some clients may be insensitive to feelings, so they may say things that are hurtful or taboo in polite conversation, such as commenting that someone looks "fat" or sharing a personal conversation with others. Because the client has a different comprehension of what he or she can or cannot say, this can lead to misunderstandings. It is important for job coaches to speak to employers about such possibilities when they are placing developmentally disabled individuals with special communication limitations, so that both the employer and their employees can understand and accept these limitations and go on to work more successfully with that person.

- **Dealing with Bullying and Discrimination.** In some jobs, the client may face bullying and discrimination from other workers, or from customers if the client is in a position that involves customer contact. Staffers should discuss this possibility when making a job placement so that the employer can help to prevent bullying or discrimination against the client once he or he is on the job. *THIS IS A KEY OBSERVATION POINT, EVEN DURING JOB ASSESSMENT.* At the same time, the staffer should help prepare the client for the possibility of bullying and discrimination, and speak with them about how to react if co-workers treat them badly. For example, the client might speak to their employer, or they might meet one-to-one with someone who is acting inappropriately to see if that can promote understanding and acceptance before getting the employer involved. Alternatively, if the bullying and discrimination are coming from a customer, the employee should be advised to discuss this with the employer, who can deal with that customer and resolve the problem.

- **Helping the Client Deal with Social Issues.** Another factor to consider when preparing a client to start a new job is the kind of social issues they may face. For example, some social issues may come up when the employee is from a different ethnic or cultural group; the employee must understand possible issues that may arise due to such differences. At the same time, these concerns should be discussed with the employer to promote understanding and acceptance among co-workers, clients, and customers.

Different Ways to Gain Experience in One's Chosen Field

While getting a placement in paid employment might be one desirable option, there might be times when a developmentally disabled individual is encouraged to gain experience in a particular field by volunteering or participating in an internship or apprenticeship. Such an internship or apprenticeship may or may not be paid, or be paid at a small wage; the compensation may be much lower than an individual might normally receive for doing that work, but it can provide the client with new skills that can help them get a better-paying job in the future.

While interviewing a client to learn about their interests and abilities, a staff member might explain these opportunities and show how being a volunteer, intern, or apprentice can be a stepping-stone to getting a paid job later on. Here is how a staff member might describe such an opportunity—for example, a volunteer opportunity.

Volunteering can be a terrific way to learn about your interests and abilities before paid employment. Many organizations offer volunteer opportunities where there is no pay. It is a valuable way to learn from different experiences about what you can do and like to do, as well as what you do not like doing, so that you will not seek employment in a field you do not like. It can be especially valuable to get a letter of recommendation from a supervisor after a good volunteer experience, since such a reference can contribute to getting a paid position. Then, too, it is important to update one's resume after each work opportunity, so it is always current.

Rise Staffing partnered with Centenary United Methodist Church to do just this. The Deaconess Melanie Dewey developed job descriptions for the volunteers, and the volunteers can do tasks around the church that need to be done. One task involves helping with Centenary Chic, a closet filled with donated clothing. The volunteers sort, hang, fold, iron, and sometimes even help sew the garments. This church is downtown, and we have a lot of homeless people in the area. People who are in need near the church come in and shop in Centenary Chic, giving our clients some social interaction while learning retail customer service skills.

Also, Centenary has hosted Meals on Wheels volunteers, so our clients have been able to help with that program, too. Meals on Wheels volunteers often stay and spend time with our clients—doing things like playing piano, making cookies, or just having lunch. The best thing is that we sometimes get job leads from these volunteers after they see the abilities of our clients. It can be great for our POD volunteers to work together with other volunteers like this. In a way, they were applying for jobs while volunteering. Job developers kept them in mind, and would come in to discuss the current openings. One day a guy who we have known since kindergarten declared he wanted a particular job. What? You never wanted to work a day in your life, are you sure? Yes, he said, and then set off with his coach to prove he was ready. I called this POD a job factory!

One of our ladies went down the street to a local elementary school to be a volunteer reader. She learned about a lot of things that the school needed. She was able to bring this experience back to the Deaconess, which helped them grow the community outreach program. Because of this, the lady was offered and accepted a part-time outreach job with Centenary United Methodist Church.

Other ways to find jobs include networking and researching companies to find out what jobs are available. In some cases, clients with more social and cognitive skills can engage in these activities in order to help both themselves and other clients, while staff members can also use these methods to find job opportunities. I will describe each of these approaches to finding jobs in more detail.

Finding Job Opportunities through Networking

There are two types of networking: in-person and online. At one time, most networking occurred through in-person events, from social gatherings to meetings and conferences; increasingly, networking is occurring online, so clients and staffers might consider either doing both, or using the approach that feels most comfortable for them.

Networking can be especially valuable for finding out about jobs that are not publicly advertised—about 80 percent of them, according to Cornell University's Career Center. Networking can be one way to learn about these job opportunities that are not promoted or are not yet advertised. For example, such opportunities can occur for both new positions and for openings due to someone leaving a job that now must be filled.

One kind of networking that both clients and staffers can use involves tapping into one's personal network, including family, friends, neighbors, and associates at current and past positions. Besides reaching out to their contacts, staff members can meet with clients individually or in a support group and let them know to ask their contacts for any job leads.

Secondly, networking often occurs at organized events, from social and business meetings to conferences, workshops, seminars, and lectures. Typically, times for networking are scheduled before and after the meeting and at breaks during the event.

At these times, it is good to have a prepared approach for meeting with people at the event, such as a fifteen- or thirty-second "elevator pitch" designed to quickly state who you are and what you are looking for. You can move on from individual to individual, collect cards or write down contact information, and plan to follow up later. There is something of an art to making the most of networking, though these skills can be learned. Some books on how to network effectively have become classics, such as *How to Work a Room* by Susanne RoAne. Besides learning how to do effective networking themselves, staff members can teach clients with the appropriate social and cognitive skills how to network, too.

There are also a growing number of online social networking sites where both clients and staff members can meet others online. Some of these sites include LinkedIn, Facebook, Instagram, and TikTok. In addition, some organizations put on various networking events or provide a platform for others to create such events, such as Meetup. Plus, many business organizations sponsor networking activities, such as the Chamber of Commerce in cities around the U.S., service organizations such as the Rotary Club, and new networking groups that have sprung up that link people with certain skills or who work in certain businesses. To conduct these networking groups, facilitators use platforms like Zoom, Blitzr, Google Meet, and GoTo Webinar.

It can take some time to find the best online networking groups and platforms, but they all generally use several types of online technology tools to enable people to communicate easily via the internet to share information and resources. Often these get-togethers are linked together by a speaker or an introduction by the facilitator. Then, there are typically break-out rooms in which smaller groups of individuals—commonly about six to eight people, though they can be smaller or larger—join for ten to fifteen minutes and share about who they are, offer insights on careers, or give each other advice. While individuals commonly sit in front of their computer and speak using their computer's microphone, individuals can also share information via an online chat and use screen sharing to show videos, images, links to podcasts, and other multimedia.

Because online social networking involves some training on how to use technology and communicate on the internet, it can be helpful for staff members to learn how to use this networking approach first, and then share it with clients who feel comfortable learning and using this approach to communicate with others.

Creating a Resume and Other Materials for the Job Seeker

As with any job, a resume is important. A printed resume can include detailed information about the job seeker organized in several ways. Lately the use of video resumes has been on the rise; these resumes feature the candidate's career highlights in a thirty-to-sixty-second pitch.

I will now describe some basic features of both types of resume, along with some strategies for creating them.

Creating a Print Resume

A print resume should always include the following information about the job seeker, though the document can be organized and formatted in a variety of ways in order to increase visual appeal and catch employer interest. A staff member can help a client acquire the necessary information, and if the client is not able to compose the document on their own, the staff member can do it on their behalf.

The basic sections of a print resume include:

- Name and contact information
- Job objectives (which can be adapted to feature different objectives when applying for different jobs)
- Experience, organized with the most recent experience first; if the job seeker has experience in several types of jobs, their experience might be broken into categories and then presented in reverse chronological order (that is, with the most recent experience first) within each category. Sometimes a resume may only list experience relevant to the position they are applying for, while leaving off unrelated experience. For example, if the job seeker is looking for a job in sales or as a greeter, that kind of experience might be included, while the job seeker's experience doing factory work or manual labor could be omitted. The type of experience and job title should be listed, along with the dates they started and ended the position, followed by a short one- or two-sentence description of the work.
- Education, listing the schools the job seeker has attended and any degrees obtained; this section might also include special training or certificates.
- References, listing the names, titles, companies, and contact information of the individuals giving the reference,

followed by a sentence or two from that individual describing their experience with the job seeker.

If a job seeker has limited education or experience due to a disability, this may be noted and explained on the resume. For resumes written in the traditional style, which follows a fixed, formulaic presentation, this information would come at the beginning, right after the job seeker's name.

Today, however, it is often better to submit a resume that is more visually appealing. One approach is to include a photo of the job seeker in one column on the left, followed by a summary statement describing what the job seeker is looking for and highlights of the job seeker's relevant experience or education. The right section includes a more detailed presentation of the person's experience and education, along with their contact information. There are fewer limitations on how modern resumes can be formatted, and job seekers can get creative when coming up with dynamic ways to present their information.

Once the printed resume is created, it can be saved as a PDF. The PDF can be used in numerous ways. It can be printed out to hand to an employer during an interview. It can be emailed to an employer as part of an application, or sent before or after an interview. It can be uploaded to a website or job connection site. It can also be uploaded, attached to, or copied and pasted into an email or online application.

While many job seekers can do much of this resume distribution themselves if they are able to, a staff member can also use these resumes in the process of looking for jobs on behalf of clients.

Creating a Video Resume

A video resume can be a powerful tool for presenting the skills and experience of the job seeker, along with providing dramatic examples of the person at work. The result can be a much more personal presentation of the job seeker and can provide a compelling sales pitch for why the person may be a good fit for the job.

One type of video resume can feature highlights drawn from a printed resume. Another can feature video testimonials about how well the job seeker has performed either in work settings or in a classroom or training environment. Video resumes can also combine elements of both approaches.

While a simple video resume can sometimes be created using a phone's camera held horizontally, it is best to bring in a professional videographer to create a strong visual presentation. Once the video is created, it can be uploaded onto a YouTube channel or a website, or it might be emailed to a prospective employer directly.

Let me share a story with you to show you the power of video resumes. I once worked with a client named Laurie who had many skills; I knew she could do anything she decided to. The trick was to convince others that this was true. I accompanied her many times as she approached potential employers, which she usually did in person since she was targeting businesses within walking distance of her home, as she did not drive. It was discouraging for Laurie to be turned down when approaching employers in person.

One day we set out for another job search, planning to visit the Hilton Garden Inn in Broken Arrow. I asked her if she ever prayed. Laurie said, "Sure I do." So she made a sweet prayer, and at the end said, "And please, don't have them put me off." Previously we had made a video resume for Laurie. It included her doing hotel cleaning work, among other tasks she can do. Before we walked into the hotel, we discussed using the video; I then gave Laurie our iPad and queued up her video.

Laurie walked to the front desk, where Amy was on duty. Amy said she would give her information to the housekeeping manager, but Laurie added, "Oh, would you like to see my video resume?" Amy said she would. After she watched it, Amy went to get the housekeeping supervisor, who gave Laurie an immediate interview.

As we were walking out after the interview, it was not clear if Laurie would get the job. I noticed Laurie's head bent down low, so I said to her, "It's okay, you are not being put off." Just then, as if she heard us, Dorothy, the housekeeping supervisor, said, "Laurie, I am not putting you off, I am deciding the best place for you to work here at HGI."

Honestly, Laurie and I almost screamed with excitement—but we managed to wait till we got outside! As of this writing, Laurie is going into her fifth year of employment.

CHAPTER 9
Helping The Disabled Do The Job

Once a developmentally disabled client is placed in a job, our assistance does not end. Instead, clients are provided with instructions and some hands-on guidance on how to do the job. Indeed, it's common for employment agencies and recruiters placing able-bodied employees in jobs to provide some assistance in order to help that person remain on the job and thrive. But our on-the-job assistance for developmentally disabled clients commonly goes further. For example, it can include printed or video instructions on how to do the job. It may also aid with social and language skills, so the client can better relate to others in the workplace, better understand instructions, and better communicate with others about the work.

Creating a Guide for Daily Work Instructions

For a good example of how this works, let's take a look at the detailed instructions that one of our clients, Adrian, was given regarding how to do his job as a greeter at the Tulsa Drillers minor league baseball stadium. We created this Daily Work Instructions guide for both Adrian and the staffer assisting him. Apart from the work instructions, this guide included photos to make it more interesting to readers.

Some of the features of the guide include:

- Information for the staffer on how to get Adrian to his workplace and what he should wear at work
- Where to go once at the workplace
- What Adrian should do once there
- Adrian's boss and supervisor

Adrian Daily Work Instructions

On Game Day, Adrian needs to be at Drillers Stadium one hour and fifteen minutes before the first pitch. Adrian and coach must be in uniform. Uniform is a dark blue Drillers shirt and khaki pants or shorts and a Drillers name badge.

Nicole is the gatekeeper; she will let you and Adrian in. Note: Only Adrian and his job coach are admitted with no fee. Any other attendees need to have a ticket for entry. Persons with a ticket may enter at the same gate—

 however, they do not have suite access.

Enter the Stadium and go to the Guest Service Booth on your right side. Look for the time clock issue sheet on a clipboard and sign Adrian in for his shift. You do not need to put your name down, only Adrian's.

Go into the First Aid door to the right of this booth. There are restrooms on the left side. After you pass a drink machine you will find the Game Day Sheet. Take one and proceed to the Suite entry. Different people man this area, but they know Adrian and will let you both onto the elevator. You can get a drink from this area during Adrian's shift.

Adrian's Position

Be sure to stay on his right side so he can do his job greeting and directing the fans. Set up his Tobii device and assure his gaze is catching the desired communication. Time the gaze-to-speech to assist Adrian in greeting fans.

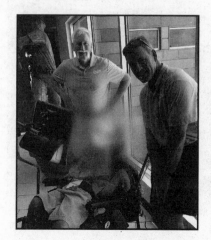

Dale and Jeff Hubbard
Drillers Owners

Mike Melega
Drillers General Manager, Big Boss

Ree, Co-Worker
and Deck Food Supervisor

Cameron, Supervisor

Adrian can take a break from the 3rd to the 8th inning. Adrian can watch the game in an empty suite, or down on the concourse on the third baseline. At this time, you may get a snack at half-price and a free drink in the first aid hall.

In the 8th inning, Adrian is placed on the opposite side and his Tobii is on screen two, which has his farewell greetings. Once the fans are all out of the suites and Cameron gives the go-ahead, Adrian will need to sign out at the Guest Service Booth. If the booth is closed, we will need you to let Cameron know his sign-out time.

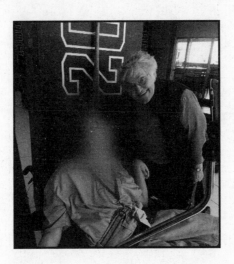

PART II

THE POSITIVE IMPACT

CHAPTER 10

Creating A Radio Show About People With Developmental And Other Disabilities In The Workforce

In April 2021 I created a radio show that features interviews with individuals who have been helping the developmentally disabled, and with members of the disabled community who have succeeded in different areas of life. It is called *The Hidden Workforce*.

I started the show when I was in the Tulsa Chamber of Commerce, where I was part of a Chamber referral and networking group that met regularly. Through this group I met Darryl Baskin. We became good friends after working together on a number of projects for the Chamber. One especially memorable project was a CEO roundtable, in which a group of us met for lunch with the CEOs of a variety of companies. During these meetings, some peers became mentors for others—which is what Darryl did for me.

Darryl always inspired me because when he was young, at a time when people were reluctant to go into real estate, he decided that was the career for him. At first, no one would take him seriously, but a realtor named Barbara Mooney took Darryl under her wing, and Darryl started his career in real estate. He soon started some unique ways to promote his business and get clients. One was creating videos of the houses that he had for sale and running the videos on Sunday morning television, before the churches held their services. He also started a radio show on our local KRMG station. He called the show *The Market Expert Hour*, and it was so successful that it has been going on for over fifteen years.

The inspiration for my show began when Darryl called me one day and asked if I would like to be interviewed for his radio show. Of course, I said yes right away. On the show, I talked about what I did for a living.

Since I enjoyed talking to Darryl during the interview, I asked him how to do a radio show. How does it work? Do you have to pay to be on the air? He said, "Yes, you do have to pay, but I get sponsors that help me offset the cost."

Before I spoke to Darryl, a lot of my friends told me that I should do a blog or create a YouTube channel featuring stories from the work I do, talking about my interesting experiences and those of my clients. I never got around to creating a blog or YouTube channel, but after speaking with Daryl about how to do a radio show, I thought I could do this instead.

When I told Darryl I was interested, he said he would help me, and we agreed on a price and a time slot for the show—twenty-one minutes of airtime on Saturday at 9 a.m. and on Sunday at 3 p.m. I decided to call my show *The Hidden Workforce*, and make it about the positive impact that people with developmental and other disabilities make on the workforce. Since then, I have had all kinds of guests on the show; my most famous and favorite guests are the people that I provide services to, most notably Charles "Chuck" Baldridge, who was on *Dallas*.

My first shows were recorded and edited by Darryl in his studio; later, I bought some microphones to do it myself. At first, I experienced some difficulty getting the audio to record properly, so I had to rerecord it. I was initially nervous and not sure what I would talk to guests about, so I found a helper on Fiverr, a service that connects people to others offering services all over the world. That is where I met Shani from Sri Lanka, who wrote up my interview questions, which I gave to my guests before we recorded the show. The guests liked getting the questions because it gave them time to prepare a list of responses.

Yet whenever a guest joined me to do the show, we rarely followed the script, because our discussion about the hidden workforce became more like a conversation, with the questions as a helpful guide to keep us relaxed. It was also extremely helpful to have a support system across the world in Shani. She was even a guest on the show and is still writing, though she will be working with Air Qatar soon. Over the years we have become friends, though we've never met in person.

I also used Fiverr for help in fixing some audio recordings to take out extraneous sounds, and I made another friend on Fiverr, Diane Davis, who does my commercials for me; listeners will hear her voice announcing various products and services available to them. Then, after I briefly signed up for a class at Tulsa Tech, which turned out to be about making an album rather than doing a radio show or podcast, the instructor gave me some tips and contacts. One of them was the owner of the radio station 105.7 FM, Jason Bennett, who came out to the studio and showed me how to get a better-quality recording of the show.

Now that I am continuing to do the show, I have found it a fantastic way to be involved with wonderful people around the world. I found it especially uplifting when I was cooped up at home for about three months after having neck surgery and was stuck in a neck brace. Then, too, the radio show is a way I can report on how I have continued to help people get jobs. I believe we are making a difference by airing their stories and successes on *The Hidden Workforce*. It is as if this radio show is the culmination of my early dream of dedicating myself to my life mission of helping the developmentally disabled live better lives, which includes finding work that makes them happy and which they can do well.

Special Guests

While producing this show I have met many inspiring guests, and I have been especially inspired by the stories of some of the developmentally disabled guests who have joined me. Here are the stories that I found especially moving:

Randall McGoffin and Coaching the Special Olympics

During our interview, Randall McGoffin described how he was inspired by the kids he coached for the Special Olympics. He grew up in the 1950s in a middle-class family in a neighborhood with many children. He attended a nearby Catholic elementary school with his two brothers. In fourth grade, he became especially enamored of baseball, though he liked other sports, such as basketball, football, and foot racing. He even imagined becoming a big-league ball player like Stan "the Man" Musial of St. Louis Cardinals fame. As a result of his interest, he was driven by the challenge of competition to become the best player that he could be. Besides his love of playing the game, he loved winning, so he combined sportsmanship with a strong competitive drive.

Then, his smug notions about sportsmanlike competition were upended when he met a young man in a wheelchair one afternoon in Tulsa, Oklahoma. This encounter occurred after McGoffin had served for four years in the Navy and went through the Speech-Language Pathology undergraduate and graduate programs at the University of Tulsa. After leaving the university, he launched a thirty-seven-year career in public schools as a speech-language pathologist and special education administrator in two different school districts in the Tulsa area. In one district, he became involved in the Special Olympics, which seemed like a natural connection due to his background as an athlete and his love of sports.

He began coaching special needs students to prepare them to participate in the Special Olympics and quickly earned the title "Coach." But in his second year of involvement in the Special Olympics, he learned that he had been operating under false pretenses regarding competition and sportsmanship.

He discovered this one spring day when his team was invited to an area meet at a West Tulsa high school. The athletes were decked out in their school uniforms and ready to perform. One of the events was a wheelchair slalom race in which participants must maneuver in and out of a line of cones for fifty yards. As a coach, he was assigned to assist in this event.

The race was about to begin, with the entrants racing against the clock for the best time. Only two competitors could race at a time because each lane took up so much room, so several heats were scheduled to accommodate all the entrants.

It was time for the last heat, with two athletes in wheelchairs eager to race. The racers waited, the gun was fired, and they were off! One jumped out to a quick lead, easily maneuvering through the course. After he crossed the finish line and gained the first-place medal, he excitedly pumped his fists in the air, shouting about his wonderful performance.

Meanwhile, the other racer was still back near the starting line, struggling toward the first cone. Upon seeing this from the finish line, the winner quickly wheeled back to the other racer, grabbed the arm of his wheelchair, and dragged him through the slalom to the finish line. When they crossed the line, they both celebrated their victory.

Seeing this display of support by the winner, McGoffin described how this experience transformed him. As he put it, "I stood with a lump in my throat and a tear in my eye. Before then, I thought I knew everything about competition and sportsmanship, but I realized I knew nothing, because these two young boys taught me more about true competition and real sportsmanship than I could ever have taught them. While I could only talk about it, they lived it, and I will never forget this experience of how life should be.

"This experience also led me to realize that *I* was the student, despite my years as a student clinician at the speech and hearing clinic at the University of Tulsa and my thirty-seven years in the public schools, where I worked with many special needs students. Those special needs individuals taught me more about what matters in life than I could imagine."

McGoffin also witnessed other displays of inspired human behavior during his thirty-seven years in public schools, as a special educator who participated in over fifteen thousand parent/teacher conferences. These displays of behavior helped to reveal how much individuals could do despite their disabilities, which had a significant impact on his professional and personal life.

One incident was especially touching for him. It happened while he worked in a public school as a speech-language pathologist in the late 1970s. He had been hired in accordance with a federal law that provided a complete range of services for students with disabilities. As a speech and language specialist, he was a part of the multi-disciplinary educational team at each of the district's sites.

In one of the elementary schools, a childless couple in the district adopted two young children, who both came from abusive backgrounds. The adoptive parents, whom I will call the Smiths, were very sincere, religious people who wanted to provide a wholesome home for these two youngsters. But after the children entered the school system, it became clear that one of them, whom I will call Mary, had special needs. An initial assessment of her skills suggested probable cognitive deficits requiring a further assessment, and the

Smiths agreed to a recommended thorough evaluation of Mary and her educational needs.

The results of a multidisciplinary evaluation, including a psychoeducational assessment, indicated that Mary needed special education services based on her cognitive and educational achievement levels, which showed a severe intellectual disability. Additionally, she needed speech and language services.

The educational team met and developed an educational plan for Mary, which included placing her in a self-contained special education class and providing speech and language therapy twice weekly. Then, the team had the challenging task of telling the parents that their child had an intellectual disability, meaning that she did not have "normal" reasoning skills and would have many academic challenges throughout her experience of the educational system. Accordingly, the team planned to present its educational recommendations to the parents. A meeting with them was scheduled to review the evaluation results, explain the suggested course of action, and complete the necessary paperwork so that Mary could begin receiving special education services.

Such conferences can be very intimidating to parents, because of the large number of team members at the table, and the meeting with Mary's parents was no different. At the meeting, there was a regular classroom teacher, a special education teacher, a speech-language pathologist, a psychometrist (who conducts the ability and achievement testing), a counselor, a special education administrator, and the building principal; the Smiths were outnumbered seven to two.

The team members then explained the evaluation results in detail as the Smiths listened patiently. But when they described Mary's intellectual deficits, the parents, and especially Mrs. Smith, bristled, indicating they were not ready to accept the diagnosis. Though all the professionals at the table attempted to convince them that the evaluation accurately depicted Mary's ability, achievement, and language levels, the Smiths refused to sign the necessary papers for Mary to begin receiving the educational services she needed to succeed in school.

Why not? In the end, after much back-and-forth discussion, Mrs. Smith stood up and announced, "We believe in miracles, and we have turned Mary over to the Lord."

At that point, all the professionals at the table fell silent, their heads lowered in defeat, except for the special education teacher who spoke up firmly. "Mrs. Smith, I believe in miracles, too," she said. "And I believe that it is a miracle that God put me on this earth to teach your child."

At once, the Smiths relaxed and signed the papers. After that, Mary's journey to receive the education and support she needed began.

Having spent 37 years in public schools as a special educator and having participated in approximately 15,000 parent/teacher conferences, I had the opportunity to witness some phenomenal displays of inspired human behavior. Some of those had an enormous impact on my professional and personal lives. If you have a couple of minutes, I'd like to share one of those incidents with you. Perhaps it will touch you as much as it touched me.

The public school in which I was employed as a speech-language pathologist in the late 1970's provided (as in accord with the federal Public Law 94-142) a complete range of services for students with disabilities. As a speech and language specialist, I was a part of the multidisciplinary educational team at each of the district's sites. This story took place at one of the elementary buildings in which I served. A childless couple in our district adopted two young children, both of whom had abusive backgrounds. I will call the student at the center of my story "Mary". I will call the adoptive mother "Mrs. Smith". The adoptive parents were very sincere, religious people who wanted to provide a wholesome home for these two youngsters. Upon entry into our school system, it was evident from day one that Mary was a student with special needs. A cursory assessment of her skills indicated probable cognitive deficits that would require further assessment. When we recommended a thorough evaluation of Mary and her educational needs, the parents agreed and signed the necessary papers. A multidisciplinary evaluation was conducted including a psychoeducational evaluation which revealed Mary's cognitive and educational achievement levels. The results of the evaluation indicated that Mary was in need of special education services. Her cognitive levels were in the range of an intellectual disability (previously referred to as "mental retardation"). She needed speech and language services as well. The educational team met and developed an educational plan which included placing Mary in a self-contained special education class and providing speech and language therapy twice weekly. A conference was scheduled and the stage was set to put Mary on a track of improvement and success.

One of the most difficult responsibilities as a special educator is to inform a parent that their child has an intellectual disability. This means explaining that their child does not have "normal" reasoning skills and will have many academic challenges traveling through the educational system. Well, that was indeed the task that our multidisciplinary team faced with Mr. and Mrs. Smith. The meeting was scripted as a result of the team staffing, and team members felt confident about the educational recommendations to be presented to the parents.

With the educational plan having been developed, the parent meeting was scheduled so as to review the evaluation results, explain the suggested course of action, and complete the necessary paperwork so that Mary could begin receiving special education services.

Those conferences could be very intimidating to parents. The sheer number of team members at the table could be overwhelming.

At the meeting for Mary, there was the regular classroom teacher, special education teacher, speech-language pathologist, psychometrist (who conducted the ability and achievement testing), counselor, special education administrator, and building principal. Mr. and Mrs. Smith were outnumbered seven to two! The Smiths listened patiently as the evaluation results were explained in great detail. When it came to the part where Mary's intellectual deficits were declared, the parents (especially the mother) bristled. The tone of their voices and their body language indicated that they were not ready to accept the diagnosis. Every professional at the table attempted to convince the Smiths that the evaluation was an accurate picture of Mary's ability, achievement and language levels. It was all for naught. The parents refused to sign the necessary papers for Mary to begin receiving the educational services she so desperately needed in order to be successful in school. After much back and forth, Mrs. Smith stood up and stated, "We believe in miracles, and we have turned Mary over to the Lord". I recall that at that point, disappointment veiled the faces of my colleagues at the table . . . except for the special education teacher. She spoke up firmly, "Mrs. Smith, I believe in miracles too, and I believe that it is a miracle that God put me on this earth to teach your child". They signed the papers. Need I say more?

Chuck Baldridge and His Inspiring Life Story

I found my interview about Chuck Baldridge especially inspiring. I spoke with his mother, Virginia Baldridge, who talked about what Chuck can do despite having Down syndrome, and how Chuck's experiences have been an inspiration to others.

Chuck was born with Down syndrome, which occurs when a child is born with an extra chromosome twenty-one. The result is that people with Down syndrome have a flattened face, small hands and feet, a shorter neck and ears, and their mouth is often open with their tongue sticking out a little bit. The biggest problem is poor muscle tone. Although it cannot be cured, people with Down syndrome can live a normal life with proper treatment, assistance, and guidance.

After Chuck was born, Virginia went to the Tulsa library and researched the condition in order to understand it, since she initially just wondered about Chuck's physical features. Then, after understanding Chuck's condition, she accepted the situation and decided that her son would grow up just like her other kids. Though the doctors said that Chuck would never walk or talk, he learned to do both. His grandma's massage therapies helped Chuck start walking when he was two and a half years old, and he started saying words when he was four years old. As a result, Chuck was able to start going to school, and he learned how to interact with others.

Virginia also helped Chuck realize his dream of meeting J.R.— Larry Hagman's character on *Dallas*. She got to know the woman who played music for KBEC and wrote her a letter telling her how eagerly Chuck wanted to meet J.R. The woman took the message to the channel manager, who sent it to J.R., who invited Chuck to meet him in person. So finally, Chuck got the chance to meet his idol, and he even invited J.R. to come to his house for a cup of coffee. J.R. humbly accepted the invitation and told Chuck he would come. A week later, Chuck was able to participate in an episode of *Dallas* with J.R. He also got to be part of a soccer team in Dulles with special needs kids.

Later, Chuck's life story inspired J.R.'s brother and his wife, who were considering aborting their baby after learning it had been diagnosed with Down syndrome. JR's brother and his wife had met with the doctor twice, who advised them to think carefully about aborting the baby. But after meeting Chuck, they decided not to abort the baby. They realized how a child with Down syndrome could be lovable, like any other baby. Or, as Virginia put it at the end of the interview, "The best decision any kind of baby deserves is taking him home and loving him."

Sean Lewis

Remarkable.

Okay, that's not *all* I'm going to write about him. But honestly, my dear readers, you have never met a person like Sean Lewis. I certainly had not, until I met him. A man with a solid good sense about him. A man who actually loves his fellow humans and would do anything for them—anything within his power and ability. And if Sean cannot do it for you, he can connect you to someone who can. He knows everyone and everyone knows him. What, you *don't* know Sean Lewis? Well, that is probably because you don't live in the state of Oklahoma! Since you don't know him yet, let me introduce you to my friend Sean.

A few years back I was working with a pretty neat individual who happened to be great friends with Sean. This person turned me on to Sean's podcast, *Rolling with Sean Lewis*. Listening to the program, I at once knew that I needed to meet this man. So, Sean was a guest on *The Hidden Workforce*, and I was a guest on *Rolling with Sean Lewis*. We became fast friends.

Sean is extremely lucky to have his mother, Kyle Miller. Kyle put Sean's bassinet right next to her bed as soon as Sean came home from the hospital after his birth. Sean was born with cerebral palsy. Kyle loved him dearly and, as she raised him, she never considered him disabled. Obviously, he is, and Kyle didn't ignore his needs—but she accepted them and decided to not let them limit the way she treated him.

Sean uses a motorized wheelchair and, from what I'm told, has had mobility issues since he began to maneuver independently. But Kyle decided that this wouldn't stop her from taking him everywhere with her. Most parents I've known who are equally awesome did the same thing. One real difference sticks out, however—Kyle truly did take Sean EVERYWHERE. That means even stops at Quick Trip for a snack. Sean did not, I repeat did *not*, wait in the car for his snack—he went into the QT with his mother. Every single time. Honestly, parents of non-disabled children leave their children in the car not wanting to wrangle with the car seat, etc. Not Kyle Miller— she wrangled Sean and his mobility device into the store, because that's what other kids do.

As I write this I can see Kyle's face, and it is the sweetest, kindest, most open and loving face. And it's her regular face, not a put-on face. A real light of kindness radiates from Kyle Miller. As I said, Sean is lucky to have her, and so are we.

Growing up, Sean and Kyle continued to "integrate" Sean everywhere. Sean gained many friends and had some great experiences throughout his school years. Upon graduation, Sean passionately took up advocacy. Sean is a motivational speaker, author, athlete, volunteer, and podcaster based out of Tulsa, Oklahoma.

Wait, Lisa—did you say Sean uses mobility assistance *and* is an athlete?

Yes, Sean does need aid with mobility. But for each activity he does, he has accommodation that allows him maximum independence—a motorized chair, special accessories that allow him to play soccer, special top-of-the-line racing carts, and an orange raft.

Using these accommodations has not stopped him from pursuing his athletic endeavors. Quite the opposite—Sean has increased his participation in Tulsa's running community.

Sean and Kyle said that, ever since he was a kid, cerebral palsy never stopped him from playing sports. Sean is a member of Tulsa's incredible Center for Individuals with Physical Challenges. This center is a place where Sean and his peers can play motorized soccer, basketball, bocce ball, swim, and ride bikes on a safe trail on the grounds. The center has many activities besides sports and fitness, too, like art, and many classes for members. *Check out their Holiday Market the first weekend in December, and you will be amazed by the quality and beauty of the art produced and sold* by members.

Sean takes part in fun runs, 5k, 10k, 15k, marathons, and triathlons by partnering with able-bodied runners and triathletes who are willing to pull, push, and tow Sean using quick switch devices to attach his cart to be towed by a bike, or handles to push. Frankly, it is incredible that people can work together in what normally is a personal, goal-driven activity. Ainsley's Angels is the name of the organization that allows partners to meet and take part in races all over the country. Most great organizations are created from the hearts of people who love a person with a different ability. People who think outside of traditional methods create wonderful opportunities. Ainsley's Angels is one such organization. My interview with Sean inspired me to investigate further. Here is the link so you can check it out for yourself: https://www.ainsleysangels.org/

Sean Lewis was born in 1982, prematurely and with cerebral palsy. He knew at an early age he was given a gift to inspire and encourage people in the world around him. Using these skills, Sean has become a well-known resource in the State of Oklahoma.

Serving on many advocacy boards, organizations, and committees, he is a sought-after public speaker and host of the podcast *Rolling with Sean Lewis,* which can be found at: https://anchor.fm?sean-lewis4

My Friend Laurie

Lisa and Laurie have an unusual friendship. We met soon after I had first started the agency back in 2004, when the business was still small. I brought on a new customer, a young woman about eleven years old, from Broken Arrow. She was very shy. Her dad happened to work nearby my office, so it was easy for him to drop her off in the morning on his way to work and pick her up in the afternoon on his way home.

During that time, our company developed a little summer camp. I didn't have many customers who were interested, but Laurie was. And guess who else was interested… that's right, me! Laurie liked fishing, outdoor activities, swimming, and all kinds of cool things. We joined Campfire and went to several different Campfire Camps; I attended as Laurie's shadow. During that time, even though Laurie was much younger than me, I really liked her—period. I watched her grow and learn, I watched her have many struggles, lots of family changes, and lots of personal issues, which she dealt with on a very high level. Sometimes she melted down and had pretty good behaviors, other times she just got quiet and stayed in her room. But she had an amazing support system. Her dad and the rest of her family kept working with her. Laurie's grandmother especially loved her, and they helped bring her out of her shell.

Laurie finished her high school years and then went to work at Goodwill for a while. Somehow or other that job ended, and she needed to get another job. Well, this was the time it was going to happen! Laurie was not going to go back to a workshop or to group employment placement. She was ready for independent employment.

So Laurie and I set out together—we started practicing interviews and talked about the different skills that she had. We wrote up a resume and decided that we would try a couple of the fast food places that she could easily walk to from her home. Well, we went out to try to get her some interviews; I don't think I'm overestimating when I say it took us twenty-seven stops to find an employer that was willing to hire Laurie.

During one of our interviews, we were filling out the application and a man who worked at the business came up and told us point blank that they don't normally hire these kinds of people here.

I don't know if he thought he was doing us a favor or what. Laurie was sitting right there and was clearly listening, but the man still said all of this right in front of her.

I could tell she was very upset; we stopped filling out the application, went outside, and Laurie began to cry quite a bit. She told me how shaken she was to hear those words, and said, "How does he know that I can't do the work?"

"You're right, Laurie," I said. "How in the heck does he know you can't do the work? Because I think you can run circles around him." So we finished filling out that application and took it right back into the store. Then I called the company and told them what had happened. They said that was not normal for their business, and that they were very sorry.

A couple of days later, out of the blue, I got a phone call from a lady named Jennifer; she worked for the contract cleaning company for that particular employer, and said she was interested in working with Laurie. She invited her for an interview, but in the end did not hire her. Wow! Even after all of that trouble...

I was a little discouraged by then, and I knew Laurie was too. But we did not quit. We wanted to get a job that she could walk to, because her dad worked away from home and public transportation is not available where she lived in Broken Arrow. To take a lift or Uber would not be cost-effective, so the only option was to find a place we could walk to.

That was when we wound up visiting the Hilton Garden Inn, where Laurie scored an interview thanks to her video resume, as I mentioned earlier. That catchy video with an upbeat tune and a nice narration describing why she was the perfect woman for the job caught the staff's attention and led to Laurie getting an immediate interview with Dorothy, the housekeeping supervisor. The interview took about thirty minutes, although afterward it wasn't clear whether she was going to get the job or not—until Dorothy said, "I am not putting you off, I'm just trying to figure out where you will fit in best on my team."

This was a thrill, because her words echoed the words Laurie had spoken in prayer earlier that day. As soon as Dorothy said, "I'm not putting you off," I said, "Laurie, did you hear that your prayer has been answered?"

Dorothy looked up then and asked, "What's this about a prayer?" We told her the story. I think at that point Dorothy was hooked—because about three days later, Laurie went in to work her first day at the Hilton Garden Inn! She was hired to do room cleaning—stripping the beds, making them, and getting the rooms ready for new guests.

Part of my job was to go to work with newly hired clients to help them adjust to their new positions. I was not feeling well at the time, but darn it anyway, we had worked so hard to get this job that I just kept going in to work with her. But on our third day, I said to Laurie, "I've got to go next door to the emergency room at the hospital, but I will be back right after lunch I'm pretty sure."

Well, I didn't go back after lunch because I was admitted to the hospital. I had eight kidney stones and I was going into sepsis. No wonder I didn't feel well. While I was there in the hospital, fretting and fretting about what my client was going to do, I called my staff to see if someone could go work with her, which of course, they did. But I also got a message from Dorothy—she wanted to know what Laurie liked, because she was including her in the Secret Santa event at the Hilton Garden Inn.

That made me super happy; I figured that if they were going to include her in their Secret Santa, they must already like her and want to keep her there. I felt very relieved, and was able to get my medical care.

Dorothy has since retired, and—drum roll please—Laurie has been working at the Hilton for over five years, and is going strong.

Not long ago, Laurie and I were out having lunch, and she said to me, "I called Dorothy and talked to her the other day." I told her, "That's great that you're keeping in touch."

"Well, she retired," Laurie said. Then she went on. "When you retire, I guess I won't be able to talk to you and go do things with you."

"Why is that?"

"Because you'll be retiring, and that's how it goes."

With a smile from my heart, I told her, "I don't know about you, Laurie, but I consider us friends and I think even after we aren't working together anymore, I'm still going to want to talk to you and be your friend!"

Laurie agreed that she felt the same exact way, and now we are friends.

If you have job openings, get in touch with me.

Listen to *The Hidden Workforce* radio show every Saturday at 9:00 a.m. and Sunday at 3:00 p.m. on Tulsa FM 105.7, HD2 95.5 or groovy1057.com

Check out Rise Staffing at www.risestaffing.net

Like us on Anchor https://Anchor.fm/lisa-toth4

Update on the Oklahoma waiting list.

In May 2022 there were over 5,100 families awaiting developmental disabilities services. The legislature appropriated $32.5 million to end the DDS wait list and increase provider rates. As of today more than 1050 people have received services!